HOPE IN THE HOOD

A U-TURN OUT OF INNER-CITY POVERTY AND CRIME
WITH EMPOWERED YOUTH USA

Shirley Alarie
As told by **Colleen Adams** et al.

To all the Empowered Youth boys who have given my life meaning for the past eleven years,

You each left a little piece of yourselves with me and I hope I did with you as well.

—Ms. Colleen

. . .

To Colleen,

You are truly the hands of God at work on earth.

—Shirley

CONTENTS

Foreword i

Dave Lawrence, Jr. i

Preface...iv

   Shirley Alarie iv

Chapter 1 1

Chapter 2 5

Chapter 3 9

Chapter 4 14

Chapter 5 18

Chapter 6 22

Chapter 7 30

Chapter 8 35

Chapter 9 40

   Excerpt from one student's term paper:.........................42

Chapter 10 47

Chapter 11 51

Chapter 12 55

Chapter 13 59

Chapter 14 65

   Jerry...67

Chapter 15 70

   Juan, EY Student...70

Chapter 16 75

   Carlos Martinez...75

Chapter 17 79

Chapter 18 83

   Christopher, Mentor 83

Chapter 19 86

Hakim, EY Student 86

Chapter 20 91

Chef Emmanuel 91

Chapter 21 98

Chef Class 98

Chapter 22 104

Chef Class 104

Chapter 23 112

Fernando, EY Student 112

Chapter 24 118

Andre, EY Student 118

Chapter 25 121

Andre 121

Chapter 26 125

Andre 126

Colleen 127

Chapter 27 130

Andre 130

Chapter 28 133

Chapter 29 140

Calvin, Youth Facilitator 140

Chapter 30 145

Calvin, Youth Facilitator 145

Chapter 31 149

Terrance, Mentor 149

Darius, Mentor 150

Terrance: 152

Chapter 32 157

Laura, Mentor 157

Small Group Discussion 159

Laura, Large Group Discussion 161

Colleen 161

Chapter 33 163

Small Group Discussion..163

Colleen 170

Chapter 34 171

Chapter 35 174

Deon, EY Student 179

Colleen 180

Jamal, Former EY Student..181

Colleen 181

Maurice, Former EY Student.....................................182

Colleen 184

Chapter 36 185

Epilogue 189

Todd Bass, Miami-Dade State Attorney's Office: Juvenile Division..189

Acknowledgements, Colleen Adams 193

Acknowledgements, Shirley Alarie 196

Stay in Touch with Us! 197

FOREWORD

Dave Lawrence's expertise in early child development describes the seeds of educational disadvantage that hamper the inner-city teens later served by Empowered Youth USA.

DAVE LAWRENCE, JR.

What I've learned about early childhood development might be captured in these four points:

No. 1: The importance of parents: It all starts here.

Nothing is more important for a child's future than a caring, nurturing, knowledgeable parent. With the fewest of exceptions, I believe that parents love the children they give birth to; at the same time, I know that many parents, however eager to do right by their children, so often know so little about what to do. I am convinced that if parents knew what to do on behalf of their children's futures, most of them would work hard to do so.

No. 2: What the research tells us:

(a) Eighty-five percent of brain growth occurs by age three, meaning the most important learning takes place during the early childhood years.

(b) Thirty percent of our children are grossly behind when they enter formal school; at which point most then fall further behind.

(c) The research also tells us that if a hundred children leave first grade not knowing how to read, then at the end of fourth grade 88 percent of them remain poor readers.

No. 3: Building a movement for all children.

You cannot build a real "movement" based on "those" children, whoever they may be. It must be about "us" and "our children," all our children. Lilian Katz, one of this country's great proponents of early investment, reminds us: "We must recognize that the welfare of our children is intimately linked to the welfare of all other people's children."[1]

No. 4: The implications for the future of our beloved country.

We are a nation amid vast and rapid change. Today, already, there are born more children of color than otherwise. By mid-century, those we call "minorities" will be in the majority. It is in everyone's best interests for every child to have the best possible chance to succeed.

Businesspeople often complain about the quality of high school and college graduates, unaware that the patterns are being established from the earliest moments. Yes, we surely can and should be learning all our lives, but we must be aware that the windows of learning are open the widest in the first years of life.

We hear so often about America being "exceptional," and indeed we are in many special ways, but we also need to face up to reality. We have, as one example, the world's highest incarceration rate. In Florida, the state spends not even $2,500 for a seat in pre-kindergarten for four-year-olds, at the same time spending more than $50,000 to incarcerate a juvenile, not including the medical and mental help that is so often needed. Where is the wisdom in this?

What does it say about us that three of every four 17–24 year olds in our country cannot enter the American military because of an academic problem, a criminal justice challenge, a substance abuse problem, or a physical challenge? Educated people are fundamental to the national security of our country.

---

[1] Quotations on the Importance of Children, http://www.zona-pellucida.com/importance3.html (accessed 3/18/2017).

The power within each of us is enormous. Just imagine what we could do together. It is so fully "American" for every child to have the chance to succeed. The future of our beloved country literally depends on this.

Dave Lawrence, Jr.

Nationally recognized children's advocate. Retired *Miami Herald* publisher.

For more information, email Dave Lawrence at dlawrence@childreadiness.org or visit the www.childrensmovementflorida.org.

PREFACE

Shirley Alarie

Fate led me to Colleen Adams and Empowered Youth USA. Before we even met, I was intrigued by her story and looked forward to helping her share it with the world. What I hadn't anticipated was the profound effect she and the boys would have on me.

As part of the project, I conducted interviews with the boys and many program supporters, as well as requested an excursion through the hood. Colleen selected a young man named Andre[2] as our tour guide through one of the most crime-ridden areas in America.

Andre was awaiting our arrival on a warm, muggy afternoon at Gwen Cherry Park. His dreadlocks, or dreads, were tied up into a nubby, pokey ponytail and his preppy blue plaid button-down collared cotton shirt wasn't what I expected of an African-American teen in one of the most dangerous and poorest neighborhoods in Miami.

"Hello, Miss," he said to me, as he slid into the backseat of the car.

After our brief introduction, I quietly observed as Andre and Colleen discussed our plan for the tour. Never short on words, Colleen led their conversation, then suddenly stopped speaking.

"Thank you," she said to Andre and his ensuing silence indicated he was as clueless to her meaning as I was.

"I don't think you have your golds in," she continued.

---

[2] Name has been changed to protect the family's privacy.

• • •

iv

Andre flashed a megawatt smile. "Yeah, I took them out," he admitted.

"I love that about you. That is *so* nice and respectful of you!" Colleen replied.

The fake-gold outlined retainer that Andre normally wore over his teeth was missing.

He had gussied himself up for our meeting. His clothes, his hair, and even his teeth. I was warmed by the respect he was showing me, a complete stranger.

Colleen's reaction left a lasting impression of a caring, nurturing, and encouraging mother. A real mother. Not a program director.

With that brief encounter, I felt myself falling in love with this young man, who I knew was struggling to keep his life on track, and the woman who was sacrificing her own life to try to save his.

CHAPTER 1

From behind me, a voice called out the name the boys had given me. "Miss Colleen! Miss Colleen!"

I turned around to face an African-American teen I'd met in one of my sessions. He stood masked in the dusky shadows. The torrential Miami rain pelted his face and streamed off his shoulders, drenching his "wife-beater" T-shirt and ponytail of spiky dreads.

"Miss Colleen, do you have a dollar?" he asked.

"No, honey, they make us leave everything in the car except our ID and our keys. I don't have anything. What's wrong?"

"I was just released and my mom's here to pick me up. She's out of gas, so we can't get home," he said, then turned and vanished into the storm.

An overwhelming sense of failure erased my fretting over the food delivery and the rain.

My program isn't helping these kids at all. When they get out, they're still going back to poverty and all the things that put them here in the first place.

• • •

I could have never imagined the path life would take me when I was growing up in the late 1940s. Like every southern city, my hometown of Chattanooga, Tennessee was divided by racial prejudice and segregation. As a naive child, I was keenly aware of the strife and ethnic tension that surrounded me, but I couldn't fully grasp its meaning.

The concepts of prejudice and racially derogatory language were nonexistent in our home. In spite of the divisive ethnic discrimination happening at the time, my father was colorblind and befriended everyone. As a local radio and TV personality, he loomed larger than life in the community. His charisma drew devoted fans who enjoyed his interesting, complex, liberal, and artistic personality. The ladies swooned over his dreamy looks and captivating charm.

Besides his job in marketing promotions, my dad was a talented musician as the drummer of his own jazz band. I can easily drift back to the carefree pleasure of the smooth, soulful, and raspy rehearsals in our living room. From my spot beneath the dining room table, I drank in the beauty and harmony of the private show. The mixture of races and genders and eclectic personalities painted a picture of an egalitarian world in my impressionable young mind.

The massive African-American bass player was one of my favorite band members. He towered over pint-size me before he'd scoop me up, then toss me into the air, high above his outstretched arms. I can still hear the pure joy of my screeching and giggling.

Then there was wonderful Lilly. My grandmother's African-American housekeeper became a staple in our home. We continued to invite Lilly to our holiday meals, even after my grandmother passed away. Lilly helped my mom prepare the dinners, but she would slip back into the kitchen once the food was served. My mother insisted that Lilly eat with us at the table because she was part of our family.

The racial prejudice that didn't exist in my home still permeated the outside world. My school was a sea of white faces, the fact of which made me sorely aware of a racial divide. I sensed something was amiss, but couldn't grasp exactly what it was.

What I now know as racial prejudice confused me as a child. I knew firsthand that the color of a person's skin didn't determine whether or not they were a good person. However, beyond my front door were ugly reminders of the barriers between black and white. It was simply a matter of life in the South during that era.

Over time, this chasm alienated me from my environment. I didn't understand the mentality and I couldn't embrace it. As I matured, I came to realize that what I witnessed in my community was social disparity, and the pain of these injustices penetrated my very being.

Equally as agonizing and indelible were the demons that tormented my charismatic father. His years in combat as a young man during World War II resulted in what we now know as post-traumatic stress disorder, or PTSD, although it remained unrecognized and undefined at the time. Without treatment, he withdrew emotionally, diving deeper into a liquor bottle. His obvious struggle was a taboo topic within the family, and eventually his alcoholic indulgences resulted in full-fledged alcoholism.

My brilliant and talented father was reduced to a functioning alcoholic. He stayed on top of his game at the office, then disappeared on binges at night or on weekends. I lost track of the times we packed ourselves into the car and roamed from bar to bar, in search of my missing dad.

Through it all, he kept his outward appearances tidy and polished, by maintaining regular attendance at work and shining at community events. He perfected a facade to veil the catastrophes that invariably resulted from his binges. Each calamity gradually wore away the thin layers of my fragile well-being.

My mother managed the best she could, but by my age of awareness, my parents were struggling as a couple. The women my father attracted fueled his ego and dulled his judgment. This recipe for disaster, further exacerbated by his addiction, resulted in innumerable indiscretions that drove a huge wedge into their dysfunctional marriage.

My mother, in turn, masked her own pain with diet pills—now known as speed. Perhaps she thought if she were thinner or better, she could stop my father from straying. The only thing she accomplished with her flawed plan was further heartache and addiction. Needless to say, their relationship was seeped in supersize drama and filled with hurt and profound unhappiness.

As my parents became lost in their own self-absorbed struggles, my siblings and I were forced to adapt to an "every man for himself" mentality. Our family dynamics were copied from the pages of any textbook on alcoholism. As the second eldest child, I assumed the role of the parent by cooking, cleaning, and trying to be the surrogate mom. My four siblings struggled with their own roles, and most of them later succumbed to addiction themselves.

With many years of therapy and retrospect, I shed the resentment that had grown within me toward my parents. Although my childhood had been difficult, I accepted that my parents did their best, and I drew strength from my awareness that I had raised myself in many ways.

I realized early in life that I had a choice. I could either follow the rest of my family history or I could decide that wasn't the life I wanted for myself. I chose to forge another path for my future, even though I had no idea how to go about it. I just knew I had to find a way.

CHAPTER 2

I was painfully alone amid my family's chaos, suffering the wrath of my frustrated and unhappy mother. Repeated backlashes taught me it was safest to be invisible, so I tiptoed gingerly around the landmines. Each moment of loneliness fortified my resolve to escape my empty lifestyle.

Being an introvert compounded my loneliness at school, although a self-deprecating sense of humor earned me some acceptance and popularity, albeit at my own expense. An unfortunate early growth spurt stretched me into an awkward and spindly 5'7" first-grader, crushing any hopes for a social game.

Instead, I found acceptance in a small group of outsiders. One girl had been adopted, which carried a stigma at the time. Another friend was often excluded because of a noticeable birthmark. A lack of acceptance united us.

I hid my family from my few friends because my house and my parents were always a mess. Although I regret this in retrospect, at the time doing so protected me from the judgment I felt would be leveled against us.

Many insecurities precluded my self-confidence and my mother ensured it would remain that way. She taught me early on that my sharp mind was a disadvantage. "Don't be too smart or you'll scare the boys away," she would advise me, leading me to hide my intelligence.

Being a tall, thin blonde wasn't an asset either, as my looks became a point of contention between my parents. My father overemphasized my appearance by saying I was "pretty," which in turn incited my mother.

"Stop telling her she's pretty!" she would snap at him. "Some people are prettier than she is, and some are uglier. That makes her average. Just tell her she's average."

I was intelligent, yet hiding it, and forbidden to feel anything more than average in appearance. Conceit was a cardinal sin and my mother hammered that point home. She ensured I would not possess a shred of conceit, or self-esteem, for that matter.

One of my escapes from the oppression at home was the local community center. I was a loner there, but the lady in charge befriended me. As the mother of my sister's friend, Mrs. Green was familiar with my family.

"You know, you are so pretty!" she said one day. "Have you ever thought about modeling?"

I glanced over my shoulder to see whom she was talking to, but no one was there. I was dumbfounded.

"No, I haven't thought of that," I said.

"The local department store has a fashion board, which is a group of teenagers who model in shows at the store. I bet you would be wonderful! Maybe I can take you there," she said.

Her offer floored me. How could she imagine me modeling?

With her guidance, I applied for a position on the fashion board and was accepted after a successful interview. All these years later, I can still feel how Mrs. Green's confidence in me soothed my battered ego.

One simple act of compassion can leave a permanent impression on a struggling youngster. Mrs. Green was my angel. I was a desperate caterpillar suffocating in a cocoon. Every time I poked a hole to escape, my mother plugged it with criticisms. But Mrs. Green tore it open and released me. I emerged tentatively, but once I fluttered my newfound butterfly wings, I dared to dream of taking flight.

The troubles I faced during my youth shaped my future, but I had positive influences as well. For instance, my father's brilliant salesmanship was ingrained in our daily lives. Any community event warranted self-promotion. Maybe we would dress as the Easter Bunny or some other character fitting of a particular occasion. We were staples in neighborhood parades, perched on the back of a convertible with a toothy plastered smile and a mechanical princess wave. Despite his other issues, Dad sparkled in his element. His reputation earned him an enviable job offer from Ted Turner to launch CNN with him in Atlanta, but my father turned him down. Fear of failure kept him from claiming his greatness.

Students in my school were enamored with my father's public persona. "You're *really* his daughter? That must be so wonderful!" they'd say.

Oh my goodness, if they only knew.

"Oh yes, it's just wonderful," I would fib.

Despite trying circumstances, I flourished as a teen. Excellent grades in school secured me a position in the National Honor Society, and I dreamt of attending college.

Hard life lessons had taught me that if I didn't know where I was going, I'd get stuck in life. If I wanted to make something of myself, it was completely up to me, so I learned to be self-directed and set goals for my future.

Surprisingly, my mother encouraged me to have a dream and the courage to go for what I thought was right. As a strict Catholic, she held firmly to her convictions.

"You can't do things to be popular. You have to do what you think is right," she would tell me. "You know right from wrong and you have to stick to that. If someone wants you to do something that's wrong, then they're not your friend."

As a child, her words resonated with me. But even more, her actions. In that era, traditional men's and women's roles dictated that my mom would become a housewife. As such, she sacrificed her own dreams and desires, draining her happiness. For example, she was a gifted artist who never fulfilled her love of drawing. At the end of her life, she was left holding a basket of broken dreams. I ached for her. But I learned from her heartache, and I resolved to maintain strength of character and live the life I thought was right for me.

CHAPTER 3

The feminist movement gained tremendous momentum in the 1960s and I was swept up by the tide. Subservience to a man and forgoing a career to raise children were scorned upon. No way would a man hold a woman down.

This fresh viewpoint was diametrically opposed to the example my mother set for me. I'd watched her trying to please my father, at her own expense, and it certainly hadn't been a success. These conflicting perspectives left me struggling with my own identity as a woman.

My dream of attending college came to fruition at the University of Tennessee, where I fell in love with my college sweetie. We were married shortly thereafter. Sadly, his subsequent tour in Vietnam damaged him beyond anything our marriage could withstand and I ended our union.

After college graduation, I went to New York City in search of my dream. I dabbled in modeling before experiencing the classic scammer. A visit to the loft of a local photographer, who had promised me an opportunity to work in film, went sour. When I refused to wear the skimpy lingerie he offered, he poured on the hard sell. The Big Apple was ripe with pretty girls and he could ensure my breakthrough as long as I slept with whomever he chose. Once I saw he was as scummy as his apartment was, I left and never returned for my photos.

Disillusioned and disgusted, I abandoned my fledgling modeling aspirations and instead entered the fashion and publishing worlds. None of my emotional baggage had a place in my career and so I blossomed. My journey with Ralph Lauren, *Harper's BAZAAR* Magazine, and two French clothing designers was nothing short of a dream. I drew on the examples my father set for me and flourished while developing more skills of my own.

Once I took charge of my life, I started living by my own agenda. Through hard work, I transcended the struggle of my childhood and was able to help my aging parents financially.

I was making it in New York City, a fashion and publishing mecca. Money flowed freely. I ran in prestigious circles, where I met, then married, the son of a magazine publisher.

On paper, my life was perfection. I "married well," had a career most people would envy, traveled the world, and had the financial means to do anything I chose. The world was mine for the taking.

And yet, I still wasn't happy.

In the business world, I was a competent, commanding decision maker. But once I stepped over the threshold into my home, I reverted into another person: my mother. Trying to please a man at my own expense.

This split personality didn't suit me and I decided to become true to one identity. If a man couldn't accept me because of that, then he couldn't accept me, period. Even as a people-pleaser, I would no longer sacrifice my own identity.

My evolution to uncover my true self led to an exploratory spiritual journey. I'd been raised Catholic, although my father was Protestant, and my experiences with organized religion soured me. I'd seen Sunday churchgoers behaving un-Christian-like by Monday. All I could feel was the hypocrisy of the judgment and finger-pointing I witnessed among Christians.

Switching gears, I turned toward Buddhism. There, I found peace and comfort in a world that truly embraced individuals. I felt no gender or racial or socio-economic bias, and the experience brought a whole new meaning to my life. Today I embrace all beliefs and religions, and I'm guided by the belief that we're all the same, that we're all in this together as one humanity.

I came to believe that life is like school, and we're all here to be both students and teachers at once; that love is all there is; and that forgiveness, compassion, kindness, and empathy heal. Everything else destroys love.

It takes just one match to create light in darkness, and I committed myself to be a match in as many dark rooms as I could find.

By that point, the social disparity I'd seen in my childhood was in complete contrast to the life I'd built for myself. My professional and social circles were composed of the powerful and the affluent. Money poured like liquid gold in the lap of luxury. There was always another trip to take, a new car to buy, another home to purchase. Another $8,000 designer suit or $500 shoes. Even though I was entrenched in it, the whole lifestyle rang hollow.

I saw those with incredible wealth who didn't seem to care about helping the unfortunate. It felt like gripping your wallet that's bursting at the seams while stepping over bodies lying in the streets of New York.

I didn't begrudge the well-to-do. Heck, I was one of them. Still, making a monetary donation at an elaborate charity ball didn't seem to be the best way to help the suffering. Some people who had the resources to do so much seemed to do so little. It felt wrong.

For a moment, I'd fallen into the elitist lifestyle of New York City and all the temptations that came with a heavy paycheck and hanging out with socialites. But I knew I didn't belong there and felt like a spy in enemy territory. I knew too much about pain, deprivation, loss, and sacrifice.

I was an imposter. My whole life, I'd pretended to be from a happy, functional family when the reality resembled a horror show.

In my recurring childhood dream, I approached a majestic home, decorated in lush ivy and sitting among plush gardens on a manicured green carpet. But each time I opened the front door, a dark and creepy interior greeted me. Cobwebs glistened in the dim light and spooky noises emanated from the empty cavernous rooms. It was the visual depiction of my childhood.

So when I was among the wealthy and privileged, those who seemed to care most about clothes, trips, houses, cars, and all the signatures of wealth, I felt fake. I'd seen both sides of life. I had "married well" a couple of times and knew money didn't make people happy or healthy or even *nice*. At the same time, I also knew many humble people who had nothing but would give the shirt off their backs if necessary.

The world was inside out and backward for me. I asked myself the age-old questions: What is the meaning of life? Why are we all here? What is the point of this? It can't be so that I can get a new car every year. It just *can't* be that.

I'd become immersed in a world of superficiality and felt like a traitor. My mother's words spoke to me: *You know right from wrong. Do what's right.* I knew better and now I wanted better. I could no longer ignore the suffering I saw, and I began to disengage from my charmed lifestyle.

One of my many contacts through *Harper's BAZAAR* was Sam Keen, the famous American philosopher and prolific author.

One evening I called Sam in desperation. I dissolved into a meltdown while sitting in the middle of the living room floor.

"Sam, I didn't know who else to phone. . . . My world's falling apart. I'm lost. I've lost all my markers. Anything that made sense to me is gone. What should I do?" I cried.

"Take the tombstone test," he suggested. "Figure out what you want your legacy in life to be and work backward from there."

"I can do that," I told him.

Taking Sam's advice, I contemplated my future over the coming days. What did I want my tombstone to say? What would be my legacy?

I didn't have the answer, but I knew it had nothing to do with material possessions. It would somehow involve using my vast experience of suffering, transcendence, success, failure, disappointment, and heartbreak. Could I shape all those experiences into something that could help somebody or offer hope? I couldn't define the specifics just yet, but I knew the direction I wanted to take.

On the professional front, I was vying for a new position and my interview at the prestigious Hearst Corporation was inaptly timed shortly after my conversation with Sam.

My interviewer asked me the standard question, "Where do you see yourself in five years?"

In the competitive dog-eat-dog publishing world, the ideal candidate is hungry to climb the career ladder at any cost, like a warrior poised to draw blood from anyone standing in the way.

"Well, I'd like to be helping people in some way," I answered honestly, then watched the guy's eyes glaze over as the interview skidded to a halt. Obviously I didn't get that promotion.

By this time, my marriage was also dissolving and had turned nasty. He set out to use his money and power to destroy me.

"Take your best shot," I challenged him. And he did.

CHAPTER 4

Life as I'd known it was disintegrating. On top of a contentious divorce, the career ladder I was climbing was taking me nowhere I wanted to be.

With my newfound self-enlightenment, I switched gears. I initiated a philanthropic marketing program at *Harper's BAZAAR*, where we raised money for worthy causes. My heart belonged to the drug-addicted, the emotionally disturbed, the homeless, the abused, and the children. Fulfilled by the new path, I decided my next career would be as a therapist or counselor.

I envisioned obtaining a master's degree in social work and further narrowed my mission to work with gangs.

Shedding the life I'd built and all the material possessions that accompanied it, I headed south with one bag and my new plan. I'd stay with my sister in West Palm Beach while I returned to school.

However, before I completed my master's degree, an amazing opportunity presented itself to work with the Nelson Mandela Children's Fund in London. The goal was to create a world peace forum for the new millennium. I had to take it.

Deciding that this once-in-a-lifetime experience was more valuable than any college degree, I threw my belongings in a bag again and headed overseas for another adventure. Ignoring my dwindling bank account, I was determined to make it happen. I *needed* to go.

I worked on a project for the next two years, planning a world peace forum with Nobel laureates who were scheduled to speak on ways to achieve peace and eradicate poverty in the new millennium. World-renowned Nelson Mandela was slated as the main speaker until he canceled his appearance due to his deteriorating health, effectively ending my work there.

The experience was unforgettable even though the project hadn't come to fruition. From there, I ventured to the jungles of South Africa, where I experienced an ancient ritual led by an authentic tribal leader who threw bones as part of a spiritual ceremony. I'd stepped into a time and place like I'd never known. It was surreal and transcendent, and the experience changed my life forever.

After that extraordinary journey, I was again in search of my next step. The experience in London had multiplied the scale of what I wanted to accomplish in life. I'd originally intended to work one-on-one with children, but I found that my whole concept had shifted. I now realized that with a lot of work, I could help a few kids, but with a little more work, I could help many more.

One of my spiritual friends once told me that finding your destiny is like following bread crumbs. You really just have to pick up one piece, then find your way to the next one, and each little breadcrumb will eventually lead to your destiny. In hindsight, I spent those years picking up breadcrumbs. I knew I was going somewhere, but still couldn't see where.

So where would I find my next breadcrumb? In London or back in the States? My time in London had emphasized how American I really was. I adore the feistiness and irreverence of Americans, their fearless kamikaze-like approach to life. The conservative and proper London lifestyle is fine, it just wasn't me.

Like a plant that dies in one type of soil but thrives in another, London was the wrong soil for me. I couldn't articulate why, but inherently I understood it wasn't the right place for me to thrive, so I returned to my sister's home in Florida while I considered my next step.

I had a vague plan of working for some nonprofit, but as I started to look for employment, I found that my background in fashion and publishing worked against me. I couldn't make inroads in the nonprofit world and soon it boiled down to a choice between eating or taking any job that presented itself. So I knocked on doors in the fashion world and, with a résumé filled with those qualifications, I was offered a position at Perry Ellis International in Miami.

The work paid my bills but left me feeling out of sorts because I wasn't living my truth. Then, one Sunday morning, I found another breadcrumb in the *Miami Herald*. The article described kids in the Miami-Dade County Juvenile Justice Detention Center. The photo of rows of kids in orange jumpsuits, with their hands and ankles shackled, resonated with me. I folded the paper and slipped it into my handbag to take to work on Monday.

At my first available opportunity, I called the phone number listed in the article and left a voice message. "I work at Perry Ellis and I have some resources. I might be able to help," I said, but I never heard anything back.

Not one to be brushed off easily, I kept calling and was met with one excuse after another until I finally found a little crack. They were having a "career day" and one of their sponsors had canceled. Perhaps we wanted to take their spot?

Of course!

I gathered a group of unsuspecting coworkers from the marketing, sales, and design departments to join me for career day. On the designated date, as we pulled up to the barbed wire enclosure, my passengers quickly got the drift and the car fell silent.

"Umm, Colleen?" one said as the rest stared at me.

"You're going to love it. Just trust me, you'll love this," I assured them.

I don't believe my Perry Ellis team felt the same way, but I found my destiny that day.

This is it. The point of that journey was to bring me here.

CHAPTER 5

Once I made inroads at the detention center, I dove headfirst into a plan. After serious consideration, I scheduled an appointment with the officer in charge.

"I want to start a mentoring program inside the facility," I said and handed him my proposal. They were open to the idea and accepted my suggested plan.

At the center, I networked with respected people in the juvenile justice field, such as Carlos Martinez, the Miami-Dade County public defender, whom I already knew from the spiritual community, Unity on the Bay. As the elected public defender, Mr. Martinez was responsible for the more than 200 attorneys representing more than 85,000 state judicial cases per year, including juvenile delinquency.

With a common goal to start teaching something of value to the residents at the detention center, Mr. Martinez and I collaborated over options. We settled on a simple intervention program that involved mentorship. I contacted Hands-On Miami and rounded up volunteers to work with the boys.

The detention center is the juvenile equivalent of a jail for adults. The kids there hadn't been to court or sentenced yet. Diversion programs, such as the one we implemented, are intended to discourage a previous offender from future unlawful activity. Successful completion of a program can reduce the final sentence or even expunge a juvenile's criminal record.

Within the detention center, each resident is assigned to a particular section, known as a modular, or mod, based on the severity of the crime and their criminal history.

With regular visits, I quickly learned the process. Nothing besides my identification and car keys would make it past the check-in, so I left my belongings in my car. No pencils or sharp objects were allowed, including staples.

An officer would escort us through the series of locked doors and wait while we were wanded for hidden metal at various checkpoints. We'd wind our way through the U-shaped areas, composed of separate mods surrounding a grassy common area, which was under constant camera surveillance.

Twenty-four hours of glaring light facilitated routine security checks into the glass cubicles that housed the boys. The sparse accommodations included a concrete slab the height of a bed, topped by a paper-thin mattress and a skimpy blanket.

Rows of chairs forming a semicircle in our meeting room were each occupied by youth in orange jumpsuits. Some wore their government-issued sweatshirt to stave off the bitter cold—an intentional tactic to reduce testosterone, resulting in less tension and fewer fights.

Each week our vetted volunteers rotated from one mod to the next. The dozen areas housed about twenty juveniles each, with boys and girls in separate mods. Our program reached the three hundred kids who occupied the center at that time.

We secured a diverse representation of speakers to show these young men the array of legitimate career possibilities that were alternatives to crime. We hosted judges, poets, attorneys, educators, journalists, musicians, and artists. The students were introduced to new people, new ideas, and new opportunities with the hope that something they had heard piqued their interest and might provide a new direction for their future. Pizza and chips were additional perks.

If I had enough mentors on any particular evening, we presented to two different mods. As the volunteer base grew, we were able to reach more kids more often, and the program that originated on Friday evenings overflowed into Thursday as well.

It's easy to say the program blossomed, but the sweat equity to accomplish it was hidden behind the scenes. What began in 2006 took a solid year to bring to full fruition due to the many requirements, which included background checks for everyone involved. Once I was satisfied with the progress, I decided to create an official nonprofit organization.

The challenge was monumental. Our boys hailed from some of the most crime-ridden neighborhoods in Miami; Overtown, Liberty City, Carol City, Hialeah, and Miami Gardens, to name a few.

Overwhelming adversity was their way of life, but the boys engaged with our speakers and I was pleased to offer them an experience beyond what they would see in their neighborhoods.

One evening we hosted a speaker who was a chef from culinary giant Johnson and Wales. He'd prepared a delectable spread for the kids that would certainly be a hit. Unfortunately, the weather wasn't cooperating and I felt our plans crumbling.

For starters, it was raining. Miami rain is an experience in and of itself. Like pre-hurricane conditions, there's no way to protect yourself from the sideways blasts. Second, when a storm is approaching, the detention facility goes into lockdown mode, where visitors, like us, are evacuated in case the lights are knocked out.

Would we even be permitted to hold our planned session? If so, would our chef make it through the treacherous downpour? Would the food we were expecting arrive? I paced outside, fretting over every scenario.

From behind, I heard a voice calling. "Miss Colleen! Miss Colleen!" I never grew tired of hearing the term of respect and endearment the boys had given me.

I turned around to face an African-American teen I'd met in one of my sessions. He stood masked in the shadows of dusk as the torrential Miami rain pelted his face and streamed off his shoulders. His "wife-beater" T-shirt and dreads fastened in a ponytail were thoroughly soaked.

"Miss Colleen, do you have a dollar?" he asked.

"No, honey, they make us leave everything in the car except our ID and our keys. I don't have anything. What's wrong?"

"I was just released and my mom's here to pick me up. She's out of gas, so we can't get home," he said, then turned and vanished into the storm.

An overwhelming sense of failure erased my fretting over the food delivery and the rain.

My program isn't helping these kids at all. When they get out, they're still going back to poverty and all the things that put them here in the first place.

Chapter 6

I was collecting puzzle pieces, but hadn't yet fit many together. The memory of a dejected and defeated young man being drenched by the unforgiving Miami rain at the Miami-Dade Detention Center became etched in my mind as a defining aha moment.

The mentoring program had been growing strong for three years, but it required a course correction. We needed to serve a program of lasting value to the young men. Once they were back on the streets, they lacked options—our little helping hand just wasn't enough. In fact, it seemed almost cruel. Through our speakers, we were exposing the boys to great ideas and exciting possibilities, but they had no way to attain any of it once they were back in their neighborhoods. I'd missed the mark.

With a revised focus, I decided to move the program from within the detention center out to the communities, where the boys needed it most. By 2010, I'd seen innumerable examples of what the boys were lacking in life and I learned what tools they needed to move their futures forward.

I immersed myself into the heart of this matter for several years. The work gained for me intimate insight into the psyche of these neglected and underestimated young men, and the families and communities that had failed them.

Marie Osborne, chief assistant public defender, beautifully summarizes the plight of these children: When children are damaged, wounded, abused, neglected, disappointed, abandoned or on their third school or fifth housing . . . or just facing the damage of poverty, bleak neighborhoods, gunfire and broken glass, it's very easy and almost necessary to completely stop feeling and shut down. To *feel* is too unbelievably painful. To feel those terrible things, without help, as a young child with a fledgling emotional system is too much. It's the most understandable coping mechanism, to just stop feeling the pain.

Once a person stops feeling pain and empathy for himself, it's very difficult to have any empathy for others. The powerlessness that a child feels through age twelve, suddenly morphs into adolescence, when he develops a more powerful body, with muscle and motor skills and access to words and high risk behavior. This time is especially challenging for all teens, but the personal power for the traumatized youth often develops into a kind of entitled revenge. Nobody gave a darn about me, why should I have to feel anything for anybody else? People did all kinds of things to me and nobody stopped them, so I don't care if I'm pistol-whipping this particular stranger, who I have nothing against.

It's very difficult to empathize with this backstory when a newspaper article describes someone committing horrific crimes. But if you think about the shutting down of all feelings in order to survive for years on end and then you've got a little sense of power and a burning sense of shame and rage that led to an entitled revenge, you can start to make sense of it.

Shame is the number one emotion at the core of all violent crime. So the act of crime is its own high and rush. It allows numb children to "feel" something, not unlike a drug. It doesn't last long, but it's adrenaline and gives a sense of power. They feel like a failure in regular society, so they turn to some alternative culture in which they're pretty successful, by making two grand selling drugs, or knocking off a 7-Eleven guy, or breaking into cars at record speed.

The situations are multilayered and complex. Overwhelming, in fact. On paper, the solutions are simple, but their execution proves incredibly challenging. At the root is a culture of despair, composed of poverty, single-parent homes, and incarcerated fathers.

When you remove opportunity and hope from people, their dignity and motivation erodes. It's a basic human response. I was living this grim reality in Miami, but every inner-city community faced the same demons.

Solutions to rectify the situation exist, but society's desire and willingness to try to overcome the obstacles are generally lacking. These youth are separated from thriving cultures by a firewall. They're trapped in lives they don't want and circumstances they didn't choose. But there they are, trying to find the way out. The parents aren't working; the father may be in prison, the mother's been beaten to a pulp by life and despair. She's depressed and unable to function, or she has a job (or several) and works all the time. She's a single mom trying to be both mother and father to a teenage son.

It's a huge cultural dilemma that I equate to walking with a limp. After a while the limp just becomes the norm. People resign themselves to lives of hopelessness because they're tired of fighting and can't get anywhere. The social services system is completely convoluted. Those in need seem to be locked out, while scammers ruin it for the others who need it. It's a mess.

I'd attempted to make inroads at the political level by submerging myself in community committees and forums, but the natural inertia of all talk and no action frustrated me beyond belief. I needed action. But more important, the kids needed it. The societal motivation to really address the core issues was missing, so I was determined to do what I could on my own.

The businesswoman in me understood that shouting the injustices I witnessed into a megaphone would only alienate me and cost me any support for my cause. With that in mind, I eased back and focused instead to work one-on-one with the kids to try to empower as many as I could. My target was to move the ball down the field, inch by grueling inch, until I reached the goal line.

By cutting through the cultural divide, I intended to create as much hope and opportunity as I could so those children might have renewed life and, hopefully, a new path. Then those children would become adults who were different kinds of citizen and would lead different kinds of lives. They would raise different kinds of children and make different social decisions. If my vision became a reality, the result would be an empowered circle of life that would advance each generation.

One thing I had already learned from working with the boys was that for my program to be most successful, it needed to be a condition of their probation. The typical grumpy, entitled teenager resents being told what to do and my boys were definitely not typical. They had overstuffed baggage heaped on top of a teenager's natural proclivity to dis authority. Given a choice, they would never choose *any* program. The boys' participation in the Empowered Youth program needed to be court ordered.

Once I decided to bring a program into the streets, I needed a specific plan with two objectives in mind. First, I was a few credits shy of my master's degree in social work, which had taught me enough to know that I didn't want to make the boys' situations worse. Second, the program couldn't be designed on what *I* thought the kids needed, it had to be built on what *they* said they needed.

Pulling tools from my business attaché, I conducted focus groups and polled the kids. What do you need? What do you want? What's going to help you? Their answers helped me shore up the foundation to build upon.

In the meantime, my continued work at Perry Ellis allowed me to further expand my knowledge of other juvenile programs. By day I traveled the country discussing strategic marketing in the fashion world, and then I would scurry off to detention centers when I wasn't working. It was extensive and arduous data gathering. I compared the programs' similarities and differences and correlated that to their recidivism rates. After all, the key indicator of success was a reduction in the rate at which someone returns to criminal activity.

During this time, I became well versed in the criminal justice systems. The adult criminal system is managed at the federal level and practices are uniform across the country. Conversely, the juvenile justice system is under state control and each state has selected its own particular approach. No national board or body regulates any standards.

Florida happens to be one of the "tough on crime" states, where incarceration is swift and sentences are heavy. However, studies have shown that incarceration of impressionable youth is not an effective deterrent to future crime and should be used only as a last resort.

My program would be built upon the best practices I observed. The Missouri Model[3] of juvenile justice became my benchmark. The Missouri program has been deemed the most

---

[3] The Missouri Approach, http://missouriapproach.org (accessed 5/20/2016).

progressive and successful juvenile rehabilitation model in the United States. Its focus on rehabilitation versus incarceration has resulted in the lowest recidivism rate of any state.

Fascinated by the findings, I consulted Missouri Model experts, who educated me on the specifics of their system. The program was delivered in a residential setting, which is equivalent to juvenile prison, whereas mine would be community-based with the boys living at home. I needed to convert Missouri's winning formula into a neighborhood model.

Pulling all the pieces together, I drafted an initial concept, then consulted my mentor in St. Louis to streamline the design and fatten the details. After extensive research and education, I created the curriculum I thought would be most effective. It was a combination of what I considered to be leading edge juvenile criminal justice reform, coupled with the best business practices. The Empowered Youth Neighborhood Program was now officially defined on paper.

Next, I honed my sales pitch and went in search of the decision-makers. My years in business had sharpened me for this. Networking and tenacity allow me to find the right people by asking questions and never giving up. Many doors have been slammed in my face along the way, but I simply turn toward another one and keep knocking.

In this case, one of my contacts helped me secure an appointment with Todd Bass, from the Miami-Dade county state attorney's office. He's currently the chief of the juvenile division, but at the time of our conversation he was the chief of litigation and had the authority to send referrals to me. The meeting would be my one chance to win this stranger over.

"I have this idea for a diversion program that includes mentoring," I began as I addressed Mr. Bass from the visitor's side of his expansive desk. After our discussion, he had enough faith in the program to give me a chance.

At the time, I hadn't known how eager he was for diversion programs to address the increasing crime in inner-city neighborhoods. As a former homicide prosecutor, his role had been to make sure killers were locked away for a very long time. But his focus in the juvenile system was more preventive and rehabilitative than punitive.

Even though lawyers who prosecute kids can be seen as the bad guys, punishment isn't really their goal. Something must be done to show kids there are consequences in life, that everyone has responsibilities. Left unchecked, kids feel permitted to do anything and then they fall deeper and deeper into the system. Eventually, they end up being prosecuted as adults in a system where the rulings are purely punitive. Rehabilitation is no longer an option in the adult system.

Holding the juveniles accountable can actually be a favor to the youth, similar to parenting. There are some things in life a person can't change, and inner-city youth become disillusioned with their reality and resign themselves to failure. Their social and family dynamics are challenging, but that can't excuse bad behavior. They have to learn to navigate the hand they've been dealt in a healthy and nonviolent way.

There are many people who have very little, and yet they rise above it. With some love, guidance, and encouragement, rehabilitation can repair these fractured lives.

On the flip side, Miami had seen an increase in gun violence, murders, and attempted murders in 2015. In response, the juvenile system began reacting to at-risk youth earlier in their criminal progression, because once a kid commits a murder, there's nothing anyone can do for him. He's already gone too far. But what about reaching out to him years earlier? A person rarely goes from upstanding citizen to murderer overnight. It can happen, but more often it's a progression.

Rehabilitation at an early age can plug the pipeline to prison by using alternative techniques, such as helping the youth to be academically inclined.

The vocabulary of at-risk kids is millions of words fewer than that of their peers by the third grade, which is already a precursor for failure. (New prisons are built based upon the third-grade reading level of inner-city youth.) They don't want to go to school because they don't read well or maybe not at all. They fall behind, then they skip school because it's only human nature to avoid feeling embarrassed. But skipping school is truancy. And who are the other truant kids? The other ones who don't feel good about themselves. So they start hanging out together and doing drugs, usually starting with marijuana. They dabble in petty crimes that eventually start to escalate. They need a gun for street protection and then join a gang to "belong." It's a classic and ugly slippery slope.

The day I met Todd Bass I didn't know his perspective on any of this. Or that, under the direction of his manager, state attorney Katherine Fernandez Rundle, the pair was eager to reach more kids earlier in the process.

All Todd Bass knew about me personally was that I worked for Perry Ellis and had been vetted by the Department of Juvenile Justice to work with the kids. He was uncertain of my character or even my true intentions.

We just happened to be two strangers with a common goal, and Mr. Bass wouldn't refuse an offer that meshed perfectly with his vision. He relished the idea of starting a new program with a fresh perspective.

"I'll give you a chance," he said, and I started to breathe again. I didn't know it at the time but his faith in me would change my life and the lives of many young men.

CHAPTER 7

Todd Bass agreed to test the effectiveness of my program by referring six young men. His act of faith and willingness to take a chance on me became the cornerstone of the program.

My first boys were formed from the classic mold of inner-city poverty. Their circumstances may vary, but each story can represent a hundred others.

In one case, Ricardo[4] was one of five boys in a family created by his mother and three different fathers. His two incarcerated older brothers were the sons of one father. Ricardo and his younger brother had a different father, and the youngest brother was the son of the third father. Only the last one provided any child support.

And yet, my student has no father figure in his life. He sees his birth father about once every four years, if that. He looks up to his older brothers' father, although they lack any substantial relationship.

In 1980, his mother immigrated to the United States from Cuba. She attended the University of Miami, majoring in English. She later worked as an English teacher in the Miami-Dade county public schools until a health crisis forced an early retirement. Her household income dropped to $1,200 per month.

Most of Ricardo's friends also struggle with poverty, and many teens he knows, including his brothers, turn to stealing for cash. Most gang members he knows have dropped out of school. Murders in his community are commonplace.

In Ricardo's family, none of the three dads is actively involved with his children. This absent-father reality is repeated

---

[4] Name has been changed to protect the privacy of the family.

in the lives of almost all of my kids, and it became an obvious root cause of their challenges. This reality held true for the youth in the detention center as well as those in the community program. In inner-city neighborhoods, African-American men make up the highest prison population, leaving their children fatherless. The sons are left to grow up seeking the male energy that's missing in the home.

Few of my boys have any positive male role model outside of the program, making the relationships established within the program so valuable. During one memorable Father's Day event, we invited the public to attend our forum where a panel of boys would answer questions from the audience.

Mentor Carlos coordinated the event and selected the boys for the panel. One of the chosen was a young man Carlos had been mentoring for some time. Carlos knew this young man was struggling and in danger of being lost to the streets. Carlos had invited him to join Empowered Youth, which the young man did, and he then went on to graduate from the program and become a successful line chef at the Biltmore Hotel.

During our Father's Day event, Carlos's protégé was one of several boys onstage. As the moderator, Carlos asked the group questions about fatherhood, such as whether their own fathers were involved in their lives, and what the young men would do differently when they became fathers.

During his turn, Carlos's young friend told the audience, "When I'm a father, I want to be like Carlos has been to me. He's been like my father since I met him. Because of him, I am where I am today, and if it wasn't for him, I would have been locked up, dead, or selling drugs and robbing or other crimes."

The young men of the program crave a fatherly influence. I can't help but make a correlation to a story featured on Animal Planet about a tribe of elephants in South Africa. The normally docile and family-oriented species was found to be uncharacteristically attacking people in the nearby village. Further investigation revealed the culprits were juvenile males. The problem originated when the elephant herd needed to be thinned, and the alpha male was accidentally killed. The juvenile males were left with no adult supervision, and the result was the unexpected attacks on the villages.

Desperate to restore harmony, the rangers devised a way to reintroduce an alpha male into the wayward herd. With the new structure, order was restored and the attacks on the villages ended immediately.

This example from Mother Nature further underscored my theory that the two key contributing factors sending my young men down the wrong path were poverty and single-parent homes.

In the Empowered Youth neighborhood program, I was more enmeshed in the kids' lives than I had been in the detention center. Seeing more clearly into the personal lives of the boys convinced me the root of the problem was consistent.

To grow the neighborhood program, I reached out in many directions to garner support and increase my chances to make the most impact. With my independent nature, I find asking for help to be outright uncomfortable, but I can ask a baby for his candy if it will help my boys.

I honed a little elevator speech about Empowered Youth and became adept at dishing out the thirty-second pitch. For example, while waiting for a traffic light at a crosswalk with another pedestrian, I can now explain the mission of Empowered Youth and hand off my business card before the light changes.

I'd been groomed to spread my message through countless networking techniques. Most encounters helped me advance the program in some way, but not always.

One of my notable networking flops occurred while I was working for *Harper's BAZAAR*. We were hosting an Oscar party at the exclusive Chateau Marmont on Sunset Boulevard in Los Angeles. Among the dignitaries and Hollywood big wheels was the man who ran the LA school system.

"He can really help you with your mission," my friend suggested, so I invited him to the dinner. Once we had a chance to speak, I learned he was highly educated . . . and arrogant. With a hint of disdain he asked me, "What are your credentials for doing this work?"

Apparently he was underwhelmed with my pitch.

"Well, I'm educated," I replied, "although not with all the degrees you have. But I don't think any research has ever been done on the power of love. I don't know how much I can do, but I have so much love and I'm going to use it to do the best I can and get as far as I can and do as much good as I can. That's all I know for sure."

I tolerated criticism of disbelievers in order to find the believers—those who might feel passionate enough about my mission to lend a hand. Now that my program was in the streets, I needed a different set of hands. I still needed the mentors and speakers as the format of our group meetings would remain the same. But now that we were no longer at the detention facility, we needed a place to meet and the boys needed transportation.

Gwen Cherry Park on NW 22nd Avenue in Liberty City offered a perfect venue for our group. The facility had been named after the first African-American woman elected to the Florida Legislature, the late Mrs. Gwendolyn Cherry. Besides the recreation center we would use for our meetings, the park offers multipurpose athletic fields, basketball courts, baseball and softball diamonds, a 400-meter running track, a pool, and an amphitheater. The location was in the heart of the hood and our students were sprinkled throughout the area. Although the program was court-ordered, logistics made it impossible for them to attend of their own accord. Many were too young to have a driver's license and those who did typically didn't have a vehicle.

The only way I could ensure their attendance would be to transport them myself. If I needed to become a taxi driver, that's exactly what I would do.

CHAPTER 8

My role as transport service for the young men drove me deep into notoriously crime-ridden neighborhoods, where I was often reminded of my visit to Johannesburg, South Africa. My personal tour through the townships there had etched a vivid and disturbing memory. Fields of cardboard box tents sprung up among the feces and mud. Naked babies romped in the muck. The horrific squalor was heart wrenching.

Not far from there, we passed a bustling shopping center, where people lounged in the outdoor cafés in their fine Armani, sipping tea and head-bobbing to the Beethoven or Vivaldi wafting through the air.

That dichotomy struck me at a fundamental level. Our pets live better than those poor people, I thought.

After returning to Miami, one typically uneventful drive down Biscayne Boulevard turned into a pivotal moment. The main thoroughfare through Miami was second nature. On that particular day, however, my mind drifted back to the unforgettable scene in poverty-stricken Johannesburg.

As I waited for my green light, I was overcome by an epiphany. To my left was Overtown, which was rife with poverty and misery. To my right was a whole other world, where people were splurging in the upscale boutiques and dining at the finest eateries.

Why had I mentally berated the white South Africans when the same conditions existed in my city and most every city in our country?

We have to start here, I told myself. And everything fell into place.

* * *

Since then, I have taken that basic premise and used it to undo an injustice, as I saw it. The gap between the haves and have-nots. The have-nots were the good people trapped in ghettos and violent inner-city neighborhoods, those who didn't seem to have a chance.

But my young men were more than just have-nots. They'd broken the law and committed crimes, actions that typically nullify empathy for their condition. Their personal histories conjure a negative preconceived notion about who they are and what they deserve. But I knew one thing they didn't deserve was a lifetime of punishment. They were *born* into their situation, they hadn't asked for it.

My work to date had impassioned me on this point. In order to make a significant difference, you have to be on fire about what you believe, and I was on fire about helping these kids. I was slowly interlocking the puzzle pieces to form a comprehensive program.

My work at the detention center had firmed up my foundation. In addition, relationships I was forging at the establishment level, with both Todd Bass, Carlos Martinez and their respective staff, were building the framework. These two high-ranking juvenile justice leaders proved to be immensely understanding and empathetic to the plight of these lost kids, and that was a wonderful surprise. My original impression of these governmental offices was one of insensitivity and indifference, but they had shown me the opposite.

The boys had innumerable strikes against them, but I structured the program on a dual premise: the roots of the systemic problem were poverty and single-parent homes. By recruiting mentors and tutors, I could provide a support system the youth were lacking.

The volunteer base spanned all walks of life. Each one offered a unique contribution and perspective, and every interaction showed the young men that there were people who truly cared about them and their success. Our group meetings were structured with a topic of interest for each session, including job interviews, issues of how to trust and act, and any number of life skills.

The subject matter is a magical launching pad. The group begins as a whole, then breaks down into smaller subsets, each consisting of a mixture of young men and their mentors. The ensuing interaction between the haves and have-nots, the educated and uneducated, the straight and narrow and the wayward, forms the essential building blocks of a true support system.

Our network became the extended family that generally doesn't exist for these boys at home. The juxtaposition and contrast of lives and experience creates a rich tapestry that benefits both student and mentor.

Besides their mentorship role, the volunteers sometimes extend their expertise to help the young men personally. For example, Robert is a former prosecutor in the Miami-Dade state attorney's office, and his work in private practice had dealt him criminal cases across the country. Robert had been cruising in his successful career when his grown children ventured out on their own. Looking to fill his newfound free time, Robert was ready to give something back to the community and was referred to Empowered Youth by the former president of his synagogue.

Since then, in his role as a mentor, Robert attempts to teach the boys how to determine and make smart choices to avoid trouble and not succumb to the constant pressures they face. His lessons are the same ones he taught his own children, such as not blindly following the crowd, taking a stand against injustice, and steering away from trouble.

During one large group meeting, police officers and several detectives arrived unexpectedly to take one of the young men to the police station for questioning.

During his career, Robert had seen too many cases of people being pressured into confessing to crimes they hadn't committed. Besides that, the recent loss of that young man's mother also pulled Robert's heartstrings and he instinctively intervened.

Inserting himself into the fray, Robert reminded the officers and detectives of the young man's rights. If they didn't have a warrant for his arrest, our boy wasn't going anywhere. The situation was quickly diffused when the police relented.

At the other end of the volunteer spectrum is vivacious Lynn, who's more of an older sister than a mentor to the young men. She is a receptionist for a pediatric office that works in conjunction with the foster care system and so she interacts daily with children with shattered lives.

Lynn's Action Club is a group of go-getters on a mission to accomplish personal goals. Lynn's plan stemmed from what she felt her disadvantaged patients were lacking. She imagined implementing a self-love program within the school system, as self-love is a vital element of self-esteem and determines the quality of the relationships a person forms. Lynn felt this critical aspect of mental health needed to be included in the curriculum.

With that goal in mind, the administrator of her club referred Lynn to Empowered Youth and she has since become a regular. She's fulfilled by her interaction with the boys during the group sessions, but her greatest joy is the candid individual discussions she has when she drives them home. In the confines of her car, she interacts with the young men on a more personal level.

Lynn is sweetness personified, but she proves her desire to instill sustainable change in the boys by providing corrective feedback. She took on the challenge of addressing some undesirable behaviors of our little rebel Nathan, whose outbursts had become commonplace in the sessions. Lynn pulled him aside in regard to his unacceptable behavior on several occasions, and she was thrilled when he eventually changed. His rough edges softened and he listened and participated in a much more mature manner and with fewer inappropriate comments.

When Nathan chose to stay warm in the frigid air-conditioned meeting room by sticking his hands in his shirt, Lynn pulled him aside again. "Will you please just bring a jacket?" she asked. "No one puts their hands in their shirt. It's not how you conduct yourself in a professional environment."

Sure enough, Nathan started bringing a jacket.

Every little success makes Lynn feel she's making a difference in the boys' lives. She also realizes the difference that working with the boys has made in her own life. The group discussions aren't only geared to stopping criminal behavior, they're about becoming a better person in general.

As Lynn describes, "A lot of times we get a chance to reflect on our own lives and share our own personal stories and that's the best part of the program. Even if we don't come from the same background and haven't experienced the same things, we still relate to each other one way or another."

CHAPTER 9

Besides playing our critical role as mentors, we needed to boost the kids scholastically. For that, I homed in on the local University of Miami (UM). The private research university educates more than 16,000 students from around the world. The university comprises eleven schools and colleges serving undergraduate and graduate students in more than 180 majors and programs. In 2015, *U.S. News & World Report* ranked UM among the top fifty-one universities in the country in its "Best Colleges" list.[5]

In addition to academic excellence, the UM athletic program supports more than 400 student athletes. Ever since Miami football reached prominence in the early 1980s, no program in the country has won as many national championships as their Hurricanes.[6]

Inner-city youth typically fantasize of escaping poverty by one of two means: music or sports. I dreamt of the positive influence the UM student athletes might have on my boys by encouraging them to stay in school.

I plastered posters around the campus in search of student mentors. One piqued the curiosity of a student who then approached her professor about an internship. Director of undergraduate studies for the department of sociology, Dr. Sokol-Katz has a particular interest in juvenile delinquency. Her popular course on the subject draws a full audience.

---

[5] "About UM," University of Miami, http://welcome.miami.edu/about-um (accessed 6/6/16).
[6] "Athletics," University of Miami, http://welcome.miami.edu/athletics/ (accessed 6/6/16).

When her student approached her about the possibility of an independent study with Empowered Youth, Dr. Sokol-Katz immediately recognized how the program supported several of her favorite theories that explain and predict delinquency. Specifically, she found that Travis Hirschi's social control theory along with Edwin Sutherland's differential association theory, among other social learning theories, were applicable to the Empowered Youth program.

Because my mission meshed with Professor Sokol-Katz's responsibilities and interests, she consented to the independent study for her student—the start of what later developed into a full-fledged internship program. As such, the college students receive course credits for their participation as mentors.

As I had originally hoped, football and basketball athletes signed up to mentor. Unfortunately, their rigorous practice and game schedules limit their involvement. Nonathletes round out the rest of the group. The students may take the course for credit for two semesters, although a higher level of involvement with our youth is required in the second semester.

The experience provides the college mentors firsthand insight into the juvenile justice system and interaction with kids who have lived through it. Over the course of their regular discussions, the college students learn the needs of the boys and witness the ways their mentorship provides a positive role model the boys are lacking.

Class curriculum includes guest speakers presenting on various topics. The subjects are intentionally geared for the Empowered Youth boys, but the UM students benefit from the sessions as well.

In addition to the weeknight program, Saturday sessions include planned one-on-one interactions that allow the UM students to assist the Empowered Youth boys with whatever they need at the time. Sometimes it's help with homework, tutoring on a particular subject, writing a college application, or online research. Other times the mentors just lend an attentive ear.

The program grows in popularity with the college students each year. Almost all of their required term papers will describe the life-changing impact that working with the young men in the program had on them. After their experience, most are inspired to keep giving back to their communities.

Excerpt from one student's term paper:

I chose to intern at Empowered Youth, an organization that I first got involved with when I took a juvenile delinquency course. Before this internship, I had already been working with Empowered Youth as a mentor for six months, where I'd developed a strong relationship with the students of EY and worked this past semester to continue to foster positive relationships with members of the program. As I built a stronger relationship with the students, I developed a mutual trust that allowed me to see deeper into their true identities and life struggles. This semester has provided the insight I was looking for as far as seeing the inner-city code that its members live by.

Empowered Youth is a nonprofit diversion program that provides inner-city youth with a second chance. A majority of the students at Empowered Youth are court ordered. Instead of being sent to prison or a juvenile detention center, the boys are required to meet with the program several nights a week in order to satisfy the terms of their probation. When students initially enter the program, they are put into group sessions to develop character skills that will give them the ability to change the course of their lives. The initial part of the program involves peer-to-peer mentoring, drug counseling, the opportunity to find an alternative place to live, and family counseling.

Once the students graduate from the initial phase of the program, they are taught entrepreneurship skills that allow them to not only understand what it takes to be a productive member of society but also select and thrive in a career path of their choosing. My position at Empowered Youth was program coordinator. I was responsible for different aspects of Phase One of the program. First, I was put in charge of ensuring the boys behaved in a manner that was appropriate for the setting. Making sure that the students behaved was challenging and in many ways the most frustrating aspect of my internship. Several students were not accustomed to being held to a high standard in regard to their behavior. This was a struggle for me since I am accustomed to military discipline and have it engrained in me that an individual should always be in the right place at the right time, ready to learn.

My second main task as program coordinator was to find activities for the students to do on Saturdays. At the beginning of this semester, Miss Colleen afforded me the opportunity to attend a training seminar in Los Angeles. While I was at the seminar I learned how to plan and coordinate activities that our students would enjoy along with being accessible to Empowered Youth. Empowered Youth has had many opportunities to play sports in various gyms around Miami, but it has been a struggle to find a permanent location on the weekends. Some locations already have other organizations using their facilities during our activity times, while others are hesitant to invite us back due to some of the actions of former members of our program. It is a constant struggle to find a place that is free and willing to accept the presence of court-ordered youth in facilities that charge a hefty fee for their regular paying members. The training in Los Angeles also provided me with tools to de-escalate issues with our students. I am an individual that is accustomed to being able to control a situation; I found my ways to be ineffective and frustrating when the boys would continue to act out after I had confronted them. In order to be able to deal with very aggressive individuals, I needed to learn how the human brain worked, specifically the fight or flight mechanism. I found it beneficial to allow a period for them to cool off after an incident before I approached them. It was hard for me not to correct them during the time of the incident, but with patience, it was very beneficial.

When it comes to applying a sociological theory to students of Empowered Youth, almost any can be applied. The theory that stands out to me the most is self-fulfilling prophecy. Self-fulfilling prophecy is essentially a prediction that directly or indirectly causes itself to become true, by the very terms of the prophecy itself, due to positive feedback between belief and behavior. The students of Empowered Youth are at an age when their decisions have a tremendous impact on the rest of their lives. As I previously stated, many of the students are in our program because they are court ordered to be there. If we treat them like criminals then they will continue to act that way. There is also a struggle between who these kids really are and who they are expected to be by their peers and, sometimes, family members. Empowered Youth strives to turn these men into productive members of society while they are also being pulled by negative outside influences. In turn, we are faced with fifteen-year-olds who are expected to act like hardened gang members who do not possess any weaknesses. Providing an environment that allows the students to act their ages without the fear of being ridiculed by their peers is a never-ending challenge, especially since we have them for a lot less time than many of the people who negatively influence them.

Recently, on our way to a [Miami] Heat game, one student, who I have developed a good relationship with, hid a gun in my car after I had picked them up to attend our weekend event. Even though I felt safe heading to the game, it occurred to me that this student saw life through a completely different lens. No matter where this particular student goes, he always feels like he is in immediate danger. It became apparent to me that no matter how well he does in the program, he still finds it impossible to escape the "street" lifestyle. When I was given the chance to confront him while he was in the police car, he understood why I had to notify the authorities but he also stated that "it was going to be our fault if he got killed because the police took his gun away due to us." The harsh reality for the Empowered Youth is that they will always face the temptations and sense of belonging that the streets provide our students.

Empowered Youth is a very essential nonprofit organization that attempts to prevent first-time offenders from becoming lifelong criminals. According to Peter Greenwood, "the research is the strongest and most promising for school- and community-based interventions that can be used before the demand of public safety require a residential placement." Empowered Youth serves as both a primary and secondary preventive program. Empowered Youth is beneficial because it not only identifies the issues the students face but it gives them a way to escape their harsh reality by providing an opportunity for a bright future. EY is unique in that it also provides their students the opportunity to network by providing mentors who are successful businessmen and women along with successful college students.

I feel that I have found a passion in working with our city's disenfranchised youth. Empowered Youth has provided me with the opportunity to make a difference in the lives of individuals to whom society has never given a chance. There is no better feeling than seeing a student completely change their life around after knowing where they were at when they initially came into the program. Empowered Youth has taken me out of my comfort zone and has taught me compassion, patience, and many other valuable life skills. Interning at Empowered Youth has also helped me further develop my public speaking skills, which will be valuable when I become an army officer. I look forward to continue working with Empowered Youth while I am still living in Miami, and I will always be thankful that it was an important part of my college experience.

CHAPTER 10

My show was on the road. We'd won approval of the judicial system that had the confidence in us to send us new referrals, and we'd engaged the community as mentors and program volunteers. Team effort propelled Empowered Youth forward, but I kept stepping on the same landmines.

Most of my kids genuinely wanted to change their lives for the better, but it always boiled down to economics. Without legal means to earn money, they were drawn back to the streets.

How could I boost them over this seemingly insurmountable obstacle?

The kids needed employment, plain and simple. I'd been knocking on doors in search of companies willing to take a chance on "at-risk" workers. A few got hired, but it always fell apart.

The Empowered Youth students don't have role models showing them what working a legitimate job entails. Many of their parents don't work. The families don't gather at the dinner table and banter about what happened that day at work or how to get ahead at the office. The boys in the program generally don't have that kind of exposure or grooming.

Dialogue in a typical middle-class family may include an older sibling talking about where he or she wants to go to college, and the many considerations associated with that choice. These conversations imprint on the siblings, but they're lacking in my kids' homes.

The employment failures stemmed from the boys' lack of preparation for any aspect of the working world, both in a skill sense and a life sense. They had no idea what being a good employee meant or what it looked like.

* * *

Beyond that, becoming successful requires more than knowledge or skill. The technical aspect is a critical one, but not the only one. My young men were missing all the nuanced soft skills, like accountability, responsibility, showing up on time, being a team player, and accepting instruction without copping an attitude. These intangibles make success in life or in work possible. But the boys had no way of learning them.

In addition, the "soft" things that make people easily conform to mainstream life, such as kindness, compassion, and empathy, make a person a target on the street. Projecting softness makes my students feel vulnerable, and so to counter that, they develop a hard protective veneer that projects *Don't mess with me*.

The kids in the program need extra guidance to be able to reconnect with those aspects of themselves that they've blocked out in order to survive in the inner city.

Our process needed to extend beyond just getting them a job offer. They needed to be groomed for success rather than positioned for failure. So I began structuring our program's next evolution, the results of which needed to provide both technical and academic training, as well as serve as the boys' first jobs.

The program's structure allowed for the boys to stub their toes without serious repercussions. If they fell, a safety net would be waiting below. It would be a self-selection process reserved only for those willing to work hard. I would provide the means, but the sweat and tears would be theirs.

Maybe a kid doesn't show up to work or shows up late. Normally either scenario would be cause for termination. Maybe he has a bad attitude or he's unmotivated. I realized these boys needed patience and understanding, and so I'd give them a few chances to get it right. If they persisted with inappropriate behavior, I'd replace them with a young man who truly wanted to change for a better future.

Their path out of poverty would come through work ethic and job skills. This new phase would fill the gaps that were causing young men from the inner-city to end up either dead or incarcerated.

We launched a T-shirt line that meshed the kids' creative talents with an entrepreneurial plan. It worked for a while. But the amount of investment needed for inventory, the length of time from design to sales, and the low margins wasn't a winning formula. The boys weren't making a reasonable return on their investment of time, so we conceded that the T-shirt line wasn't a sustainable business model for our program.

We'd been starting down paths that seemed to end in roadblocks, but I believed in the kids and remained determined. It was during these repeated challenges that I drew upon the fortitude that was cemented during my childhood.

The "Cremora incident" during my college years describes it best. The coffee addiction I developed in my early teens was thanks to my mother. Because she wasn't the warm and cuddly type, there were few things in life that connected us. Coffee became one. Our brief moments bonding over a steaming cup of java fulfilled a primal need, turning my daily coffee into a sacred obsession.

Later, during college, I was flat broke and riding on student loans. I survived on the $10 a week my father sent me.

The first priority on my short weekly grocery list was a huge jar of Cremora for my bottomless coffee mug. One bottle carried me through the week. The remainder of my funds was reserved for moon pies out of the vending machine. Anorexia had already accustomed my body to starvation, which went hand-in-hand with those dirt-poor days.

One fateful morning my bony elbow knocked the brand-new fake creamer bottle off the counter. It crashed to the floor, exploding into a blanket of yellow snow.

Staring down at the mess, I considered my options.

Well, I guess I'm drinking black coffee now, I told myself. That's it. Move on.

Black coffee became my new staple.

I'd developed a kind of survivor's mentality from my feast or famine childhood. My father earned good money, but often drank it away on Friday night, so my family either seemed to splurge on steak or squeak by on dry spaghetti. I learned to accept whichever kind of day it was.

That mentality ingrained a fierce determination to make do with whatever I have. Don't cry or fret over spilled Cremora. Forge ahead without it.

My goal is to impart this philosophy on the boys by showing them ways they can turn adversity into an advantage. I can tell them with firsthand experience that bad things can happen, but it's possible to flip it around and move on. Even a loss can be motivating and an opportunity for growth.

It was this mindset that drove me through repeated bumps and roadblocks as we grew the program. Whenever we found a weakness in our methods, such as the unsustainable T-shirt line, we made a course adjustment and moved on.

The best incentive to motivate my kids to stay out of trouble and not use drugs was the opportunity to learn and earn, but what were the means to that end? I circled back to brainstorming our options once again.

CHAPTER 11

Putting the program pieces together was one challenging aspect, but there were also the daily logistics of advocating for the boys in the judicial system. My car memorized the route to the massive, newly constructed Children's Courthouse and Juvenile Justice Center. The sheer size of the beautiful structure indicates the magnitude of today's youth crisis. I've passed the motto in the cavernous lobby too many times: WE WHO LABOR HERE SEEK ONLY THE TRUTH.

One particular day, Xavier's[7] case brought me through the doors yet again. The subpoena folded in my purse was from the Circuit Court of the Eleventh Judicial Circuit located in and serving Miami-Dade County, Florida, Juvenile Division. My name filled the "witness" box.

Xavier had abandoned the program. He was a big, strong kid with the classic tragic upbringing, in addition to being stubborn, rebellious, and close-minded. The gangster lifestyle he chose drove him beyond his mother's control. He ran the streets at all hours, skipped school, and came to the program high. I'd heard from the other boys that he'd been re-arrested for a gun charge. He'd been totally resistant to help and eventually stopped attending the program altogether. It was time to call him out.

Xavier's pattern didn't surprise me. I've learned the hard way that there's no predictor as to which kids will be receptive to the second chance they're offered.

I set the ground rules from the minute the boys enter the program. Requirement number one is that they and I need to be partners to ensure their success. I assure them I will do my part,

---

[7] Name has been changed to respect the privacy of the family.

but they must do theirs. I present them with opportunities, but it comes down to the old horse-and-water scenario. I can't make them take advantage of anything. If they're not ready, they simply won't.

Every youth enters the program at a different starting point, so I consider their progress relative to where they begin. One young man arrived aggressive and hardened, but he was also a smart comedian and won me over. He appeared to be committed to the gangster mentality, but I saw in him a dim light that slowly grew brighter. He began engaging in the program discussions and his attitude softened.

Considering the headway he was making, I selected him to participate in a discussion panel about street violence. He nailed it, sharing an important insider's perspective on the topic. He had been so entrenched in his old lifestyle, and his progress had begun so slowly, that most people probably would have closed the door on him. But this young man and others have taught me that progress is always possible, so I keep my door open in a way these youth might not have experienced before.

One day I got an unexpected phone call. "This is Officer Garcia from the Northside station. Is this Miss Colleen?" he asked.

"Yes, yes it is. Is there anything wrong?"

"We have someone who wants to speak to you," he said and then I heard a familiar voice.

"Miss Colleen, I'm so sorry," one of my prior students said.

"What's wrong?" I asked.

"I got arrested, Miss Colleen, but I just wanted you to know how sorry I am. I didn't mean to disappoint you."

The deep associations of his gang were as tight as family and included his childhood friends and everything he knew, making it tough to break away. Their grip had pulled him back to the gang, like a magnet drawing steel.

We're working against the clock with these kids, Xavier included. By abandoning the program, he was in violation of his parole, as regular attendance was one of his requirements.

By choosing the program originally, he'd been eligible for Successful Completion of Probation (SCOP), a status that would vacate his charges. With this parole violation he would lose those privileges, meaning he would have to face the original charges levied against him and take some other punishment. The violation of probation was yet another charge stacked on top.

Due to the severity of the consequences, the state attorney's office asked Xavier if he'd be willing to complete the terms of his probation by returning to the program. Xavier stood at the precipice. Once he tumbled over that edge, he'd become a statistic in the criminal system and then there was no turning back. In one moment, his fate might be sealed by all the ramifications of having a felony conviction. The serious implications pose even more challenges for those living in poverty.

During a huddle in the courthouse hallway, I reminded Xavier the door to the program was always open for him. He agreed to return, claiming he liked the program and wanted to go, thereby proving that the magnetic pull of the streets can be mightier than logic.

After two hours of waiting, Xavier's case was resolved in a five-minute hallway conversation, without ever being called before the judge.

Xavier's a good example that trying to solve a problem by only addressing the symptom just doesn't work. The problem is he's still poor, he still has no father and no guidance. They can send him to a hundred prisons and it won't fix anything. It's a cultural problem. That's how the system is broken.

Xavier chose a fresh start and returned to the program. It's one last critical chance. We can always terminate his probation, but once that bell is rung, we can't un-ring it. It's there if needed, but it should be the last option. It was clear that everyone who's pulling for these kids wants it to be the last option.

CHAPTER 12

I'm always eager to learn anything that will help me help the kids. At one conference I attended, a man from London was presenting a study he'd conducted on sensory deprivation. He pointed to a slide that compared two brainstems. The one on the left was flourishing, with many tributaries, much like the network of a thriving maple tree. It was the brainstem of a mainstream child who'd been nourished, educated, and loved. The brainstem on the right had come from a child in an undeveloped country, but also represented what one might look like from an American inner-city child. The difference was staggering.

I approached the speaker afterward.

"These are my kids. How can I help them?" I asked him.

He explained that the brainstem can be likened to a paltry twig when all the synapses haven't been fired. There are many ways to spark signals in the brain that trigger development of compassion, empathy, and critical thinking. Like touching, hugging, and caressing. Reading a book or making dinner together. Helping a student with homework, while urging him to think through problems.

These simple human interactions are usually taken for granted, but they actually promote cerebral connections that enable a person to develop into an empathetic member of society. To learn that my kids were disadvantaged in such a fundamental way deepened my resolve to help them.

With this information, I tweaked the program to serve more interactive topics. The speaker had instructed me to make the boys think, so I challenged their minds more than I had previously.

In our circle discussions, we normally asked the boys for their thoughts on various topics. Too often, the answer was a dismissive shrug or an "I don't know," and I would move on to the next young man.

With my newfound knowledge, I started pushing harder. "Yes, you *do* know. Think about it. Give me an answer," I began to insist. Or sometimes when the boys aren't forthcoming in the group, I'll prod with a little stick by saying something like, "Guys, part of graduating from this program is participation, so I'm expecting to hear from you."

Everything we do is geared toward developing critical thinking. The many gaps required an army of resources to help these kids reach equal footing with their more socially advantaged peers.

But we were getting the necessary resources in place. By this time, Empowered Youth USA was formalized as a business, with a board of directors and an official 501(c)(3) nonprofit status. The program had the support of judicial system administrators, a steady stream of youth, and a host of volunteers helping to serve the many needs of the boys.

However, on the professional front, I realized I'd begun gravitating toward the kids rather than applying myself wholeheartedly in my job. I became saddled with guilt and unhappiness. I'd never kept Empowered Youth a secret from my employer, but now I had to choose between the two. The boys or my career?

Could I possibly abandon the kids?

No way!

My commitment and passion to help the boys overrode my financial sense. Once I'd made my choice, it forced what I felt was an honorable and ethical decision. I took a personal leap and waved farewell to my lucrative career. I believed my higher purpose work was for the kids, so I sided with my gut, even while my mind berated me over the practical aspect of earning a living.

Since that time, we've laid many building blocks in place, but we were still missing some key pieces of the foundation. One particular snag remained a detriment and threatened our success: My pockets were running empty. As I'd feared, my generous nest egg was gobbled up by program costs, and few funds were trickling back into the pot. The math wasn't adding up. Volunteers offered their time, but financial donations were light and state funding was a black hole.

As dire as the financial picture was, there was yet a more pressing matter. I was still losing boys back to the street, sending me back to the drawing board yet again.

By this time, I had nearly eleven years of working with troubled youth on my résumé and I'd seen it all. Boys whose family members had been killed in gun violence or kept going through a revolving door to jail. Mothers who did drugs with her children and those without the faintest clue, or even desire, of how to parent a child. I'd seen fathers who sired twenty-something children with a multitude of women. Families moving constantly with each new eviction. Twenty people crammed in a three-bedroom apartment—no hot water, no electricity, no functional plumbing. Pressure to sell drugs and join gangs. Fathers shooting mothers in front of young children. Dog-eat-dog poverty, constant anger and disputes. Each of the boys in these stories came from unique circumstances, but at the core, each story is devastatingly similar.

Family dynamics often create a tremendous barrier to successful relationships and self-esteem. It's too dangerous to be honest about your feelings because there's always someone trying to take you down. Love, fidelity, honesty, and decency are equated with vulnerability in the inner city, whereas anywhere else, those attributes create the foundation of a happy life.

I drew on these prior experiences to determine what would motivate the boys to change for the better, for a brighter future. I couldn't force them to change. It had to be their choice.

There's nothing punitive that can be done if a person didn't want to change. And teenagers are teenagers. They do what they want, no matter what you tell them they have to do—and that's in the best of circumstances. My kids were in the worst circumstances. We needed specific and tangible ways to influence their lives permanently.

The youth must be exposed to practices that teach them ways to be productive. For example, for these kids, it is ineffective to tell them they should be attending school so they can be well educated. To *show* them the importance and the possibility, we bring them to the University of Miami and expose them to hard-working, accomplished students. Through this exposure, many of the boys have decided to go to college, even if it isn't UM.

The smaller group break-out sessions trigger valuable personal discussions between the boys and the college students. I've heard many exchanges, such as, "You know, I grew up in a neighborhood just like you did. I had to break off from my friends and focus on school and grades, and now I'm going to be a chef or lawyer."

Each of those interfaces are like synapses firing in the brain. First, making one connection, then another, and another, and finally they start to etch a new pathway in that child's mind about what the possibility for his life can be. It's not just talking. It's about showing and doing.

CHAPTER 13

In the spirit of showing and not just telling, I had to instill in the boys the desire to change and, more important, to provide a pathway to make it both possible and sustainable. Led by Gandhi's axiom—be the change you want to see—I considered a new facet of Empowered Youth that would offer training and practical work experience for boys actively engaged in the program.

The booming hospitality industry jumped out as an ideal fit for our bustling location in Dade County. It's a fertile training ground for youth, as it provides job opportunities in many capacities: servers, cooks, marketing professionals, and eventually management. Another major advantage for the boys is that a lack of a formal education doesn't preclude someone from becoming an accomplished chef.

There are more than two million residents of the county and fourteen million visitors to Miami[8] per year. They all need to eat. The hospitality model seemed to be a good fit and could also provide crucial income for our youth.

Diego Molinari, an innovative mentor involved with our project at the time, suggested the hospitality industry and a new door opened for my kids. A food truck would be our business model, along with a three-pronged job development program. On the technical side, weekly chef classes would provide the boys with formal training. The academic aspect entailed a weekly entrepreneur's class, where the boys would learn the basics of

---

[8] Hannah Sampson, "Miami tourism hit record numbers in 2013," *Miami Herald,* February 27, 2014, www.miami-airport.com/pdfdoc/Newsclips_Jan_2014/Miami%20tourism%20hit%20record%20numbers%20in%202013.pdf (accessed 3/15/17).

business. Lastly would be on-the-job training on the food truck, where the boys would receive a stipend for their work.

This new phase became the Empowered Youth Entrepreneur's Job Development Program, which was Phase 2 of the overall Empowered Youth model.

Each of the many aspects of educating our boys focuses on developing skills that are transferable and applicable to life, whether the boys go to college or straight to job interviews. My plan was to prepare them for whatever direction they choose to take, while providing a solid foundation if they choose the hospitality field.

The entrepreneurial academic aspect of the program is a weekly class that follows a set curriculum and culminates with a certification upon successful completion. The course coincides with one semester of the mentorship program at the University of Miami. College students prepare and teach the curriculum, which entails writing a business or marketing plan and determining business start-up costs, while honing written, verbal, and presentation skills.

The classes are one way to open the boys' minds and pour in hope for the future with ingenuity, possibility, and an eye toward a brighter way of life. Each two-hour session is a combination of creativity and business skill–building.

My boys are divvied into teams among the UM students, where they brainstorm together on potential commercial products to develop and pitch to the class, similar to a *Shark Tank* contest.

During one such exercise, our student proposed an app to dispense pet food at specific intervals and his idea was deemed the most promising by his team. During another session, one team chose to launch an affordable urban clothing brand to compete with the trendy and costly Urban Outfitters. Another first place–winning team proposed a shiny, pearlescent, metallic-colored sneaker.

Through these sessions, we've seen a creative variety of theoretical products. Every class ends far too quickly to expand on any one concept, but I can almost feel the hope for the boys' future that comes with each of these exchanges.

After the business brainstorming, we switch gears to the individual needs of each Empowered Youth student. One might need to study for the ACT or SAT, some need to write a résumé, and others need tutoring on homework. My boys tackle their current educational challenges with their college mentors by their side. Every participant leaves each session more empowered than when they arrived.

In addition to the academic aspect of Phase 2, we accomplished on-the-job training by launching our food truck. After securing our vehicle, we caucused as a group to name our new venture. While Empowered Youth USA remained the parent organization, a unique brand and separate identity would define the hospitality business.

Vibe 305 resonated the most of all the names suggested and was selected to represent our new venture. The word "vibe" is multifaceted and meaningful to the boys. It's cool and hip and "in." It also relates to music and art, two things of utmost importance in the hood. Our area code is 305. It's our home. Vibe 305 represents us as a unified force and as unique individuals.

A brilliant graphic artist worked with the kids to design the edgy and fly[9] Vibe 305 logo that we then plastered on the sides of the only nonprofit food truck in Miami.

The business model was designed to become a franchise, whereby the boys would learn to become proficient small-business owners. At that point, they could spin off with their own business as a franchise. Different food trucks would serve

---

[9] Cool, in style. See "fly," *Urban Dictionary,*
www.urbandictionary.com/define.php?term=fly (accessed 12/9/16).

different communities, and each one would allow us to expand the number of youth served.

But that was a fantasy for the future. In the here and now, I buckled down to pull a whole new set of resources together. I needed trained chefs to help manage a business that was foreign to me. I needed a kitchen classroom. And I needed a parking space for the new truck, plus a thousand other details to be identified and sorted out. Thankfully, by this time, we had a network of supporters who were willing to help.

One of them is Sharie Blanton. She's currently NET (Neighborhood Enhancement Team) administrator for Miami, but was working for Coconut Grove commissioner Mark Sarnoff when we launched Vibe 305. She and her then-husband provided sound advice in regard to the fledgling food truck business and valuable contacts that led us to Chef Emmanuel, who has since become a special jewel.

Another distinguished chef we scored was thanks to the help of Richard Ingraham, Dwyane Wade's personal chef. Richard learned about us through word of mouth and he happened to own a company providing chefs to celebrities. When he heard of our need, he sent one of his chefs to train our boys in the weekly culinary class.

The full picture came into focus when we secured our training facility through Trinity Cathedral on NE 16th Street in Miami. The church's kitchen became home to the culinary class, which was conducted by a professional chef and included Lisa Dorfman, an internationally acclaimed nutritionist, who teaches the boys about balanced diet and healthy cooking.

The young men learn and practice the basics in the kitchen classroom, then apply what they learned while working on the truck. The set curriculum is a mandatory one-year program for students who have opted into the Job Development Program. After successful completion, each student receives a certification for his culinary skills and the Florida Restaurant and Lodging Association helps us find them permanent jobs.

On-the-job training takes place on the truck under the tutelage of experienced training chefs. These culinary professionals believe in our program and relate to our boys, so they concede to our skimpy pay rate even though they're the top in their field.

A training chef supervises and mentors the youth on each shift, in addition to the culinary role. They address any customer service concerns and audit the youth as they work, tweaking any performance issues along the way.

The daily logistics of operating the food truck proved challenging. Just making sure we have a gig was a constant juggling act. For example, the truck might be stationed at a courthouse Monday through Friday, then relocate to different events on the weekends. As our reputation grew, the invitations to venues were more forthcoming, making it easier to keep the truck busy.

My one distinct purpose for the entire endeavor was to provide training and jobs for the boys who want it and demonstrate the ambition to earn it. With that in mind, I overstaffed the truck. The chef plus two boys are all we need to operate effectively, but I scheduled up to four boys to allow them to earn money.

Lastly, our talented chefs created varying menu items that allowed us to trade up to more sophisticated offerings or stick with basic burgers and fries, as needed. This diversity became our selling point. At a food truck rally, we would learn what the other vendors are providing, then design a unique menu that stood apart from the rest. We determine where the gap is, then transform ourselves to fill the void.

This flexibility is our ticket into many venues because we can always be original. We have vegetarian items and can accommodate food allergies. At a synagogue, our kosher menu items delighted the patrons. As an added bonus, this creativity and flexibility exposes the boys to diverse food preparations.

We explore different opportunities in search of a winning formula. At one point, we joined an incubator program, where the truck remained stationed in a desirable Wynwood Yard location, but our show went on the road again after that gig ended.

Beyond preparation and serving, the boys maintain the truck's daily inventory and replenishment, a task that enhances their experience. They also learn critical interpersonal skills by interacting with customers from all walks of life.

Indeed, Vibe 305 became the safe place I envisioned for the boys to learn and grow, and far exceeded what I ever expected. I learned that opportunity is transformational. The food truck was an amazing beginning, but I soon realized that I couldn't provide enough hours to employ the thirty to thirty-five students who needed jobs. I had to figure out a way to do more.

CHAPTER 14

One of the many facets of pulling the program together was to find and network with the right people, like Sharie Blanton, who'd helped us secure our beloved Chef Emmanuel. Since then, I could always count on Sharie to suggest potential opportunities to advance the program. Her role in the community, experience with nonprofits, and ties to then-Commissioner Marc Sarnoff was a triple win.

One memorable phone call from Sharie was in regard to the national Close Up program. The flagship high school program is a one-of-a-kind opportunity for students to experience their government in action. From visits to Washington's famous monuments, memorials, and institutions, to meetings with their congressional delegation on Capitol Hill, Close Up students get a firsthand look at the American political system and consider what role they, as students, play in our democracy.[10]

Commissioner Sarnoff authorized the trip to Washington, D.C., for youth in the low-income Village West–Coconut Grove area. He raised $70,000 to bring forty middle and high school students. As the program administrator, Sharie offered me four spots as a once-in-a-lifetime reward for our top performers. When donations fell short of the steep $1,600 cost per youth, the owner of Coconut Grove's LoKal restaurant stepped up to help our boys.

To sweeten the deal, Sharie invited the quartet who would be attending Close Up, and their parents, to City Hall to be recognized by the commissioner. As a fringe benefit of attending the commission meeting, the boys would be able to envision their

---

[10] Close Up Washington DC, www.closeup.org/program/hs-washington-dc (accessed 3/15/17).

future community involvement. Experiencing their local government at work, meeting with their commission, and seeing the elected representatives for their neighborhoods was a rare glimpse into actual city business.

With this introduction to local government, perhaps their upcoming experience in Washington would allow them to see how the pieces of the democratic puzzle fit together.

At the conclusion of the designated commission meeting, the boys assembled on center stage where the mayor offered them lapel pins as a memento of their experience.

As part of my routine networking, I was already in contact with local folks associated with the My Brother's Keeper initiative. As spearheaded by President Barack Obama, the program is described as "helping more of our young people stay on track. Providing the support they need to think more broadly about their future. Building on what works— when it works, in those critical life-changing moments."[11]

Once Sharie confirmed our place on the Close Up trip, Father Grey Maggiano of Trinity Cathedral contacted the CEO of My Brother's Keeper in Washington and secured an invitation for our boys. During one of the Close Up breakout group sessions, the Empowered Youth boys would travel to the White House for their personal meeting.

The week-long Close Up experience was a whirlwind. The youth who had barely traveled out of their own neighborhoods, let alone Miami, rubbed elbows with Congresswoman Frederica S. Wilson and Senator Bill Nelson. They toured George Washington and Howard Universities and intermingled with students from across the country.

At the appointed time, while the larger group perused the Smithsonian, my boys headed to the White House Executive

---

[11] "My Brother's Keeper," https://obamawhitehouse.archives.gov/my-brothers-keeper (accessed 3/15/17).

Office in the Eisenhower building to meet the national director of My Brother's Keeper. Each of the boys had an opportunity to speak about Empowered Youth and answer questions about why they're involved and how it's changing their lives. They advocated for funding and sold the value of the program with their personal stories.

Experiences such as this one allow the boys to hone their public speaking and marketing skills. They develop a great command of our mission and what it means to them personally.

"We need to have more programs like Empowered Youth," they would say. Or, "If it wasn't for a program like this, I would have made other choices." Or, most impressive, "I have to do the right thing for my family. My mom's a single mom, and I know I got in trouble in the past, but now I want to do better." Their stories speak volumes and every chance to share them provides learning and growth for themselves and their audience.

. . .

Angels like Sharie help me provide wonderful opportunities for the boys and lighten my load in various capacities. While Sharie's specialty is the community involvement aspect, other angels work alongside me in the trenches. Most notable is Jerry. He provides another set of dedicated and loving hands that I can use to reach out to the boys.

Jerry

I met Colleen over four years ago and was immediately intrigued by her work with the boys. I was no stranger to philanthropic work, having joined the peace corps for two years in the 1960s. My assignment was in Colombia and to this day, I'm still active in the Colombia Project that was formed by Returned Peace

Corps Volunteers who served in Colombia and now reside in the United States. Similar, is my support of the Ministry of the Good Shepherd, whose mission is to help the Sisters of Mercy in northern Peru in their community development and education. Locally, I support the Saint Vincent DePaul Society and other programs for justice.

So when Colleen explained her Empowered Youth program, I was eager to learn more. My first real exposure to the program was shortly thereafter when she invited me to a fund-raiser. I liked what I saw, so I started attending the evening program and taking a more active role with the boys.

It started out as Monday, Wednesday, and Saturday and then expanded into Tuesday, Thursday, and Friday. So I've been working harder in my retirement than when I was running my export business!

Empowered Youth is all volunteer. It's very rewarding, but tiring work. I rack up about a hundred miles daily transporting the boys to and from the program, along with running other errands.

It takes a lot of patience working with the boys, but I have three sons, so I understand. They all suffer many of the same growing pains.

There are many impressive aspects of Empowered Youth, but the most impressive part is Colleen Adams. She's fueled by an unstoppable passion and a blazing fire that reminds me of my Peruvian mother-in-law. She's ninety-six years old and still fired up like Colleen is, but in regard to promoting the rights of women, as well as arts and music and other community activities. People like her are rare gems.

Every conversation with Colleen circles back to Empowered Youth in one sense or another. She can't sleep, doesn't eat, and is all-consumed because "the program needs her" or "the boys need her"—and it's true. They *do* need her. They depend on her.

It's heartwarming to watch how much most of the boys change in a matter of months. When they first come into the program, about 90 percent are very bitter because of what they feel is mistreatment at home, by the law, by the judges, and just life in general. In the beginning, they won't talk, hardly giving their name.

And then we see them change. The theoretical definition of change is that they don't reoffend, but what we see firsthand is a matter of how they act—how they begin to smile, how they look forward to coming to the program. Our method is really to treat the boys with kindness and teach them to be kind to others. It's amazing to see the transformations.

This one boy is so excited to get picked up to attend the program meetings and he's only been with us for about two months. He still doesn't talk freely during the program, but he opens up when we're in the car. I have no doubt that he will be one of the many who leaves his criminal past behind him.

One boy I used to pick up was always late. I'd give him twenty minutes advance notice of when I'd be arriving and he'd still make me wait. But he was the first one to ever say "Thank you, Mr. Jerry" during his graduation ceremony at the program. It still brings me to tears because he really meant it.

Then there was another boy who pulled some money out of his pocket and tried to hand it to me when I dropped him off at home one evening. "Here, this is to help you with your gas," he told me. These are kids who don't have a penny to spare.

It's those little things you least expect that mean the most.

CHAPTER 15

Juan,[12] EY Student

Boredom is one reason why I committed a crime, but mostly I was following my older brothers. Since I was bored at home, I started going to my brothers' house on the weekends, but then I ended up staying almost the whole summer. Once I started hanging with them and doing what they were doing, we got caught.

It was my first offense and first time in the juvenile system. In my head, I was like, Wow, I really messed up. I was thinking about school and how my older brothers didn't finish school and how they were living off crime because they couldn't get a job.

I was thinking about how I wanted to stay in school, but at the time I was incarcerated. It was the end of summer and school was right around the corner, so I was worried about that. I was in the juvenile detention center for just over a month and I got out a few days after school started.

I was almost charged as an adult, but my mom told the judge that I'm not the type of kid the charge says I am. At the time I was fifteen years old, but one of the charges was a felony—strong armed robbery—therefore, they considered charging me as an adult.

My mom showed them all my certificates from school and my grades to prove I was a good student and that I was influenced into the crime. So they didn't charge me as an adult

---

[12] Name has been changed to respect the privacy of the family.

and sent me to the Empowered Youth program. I was like, okay, whatever. I'll just finish this program and be done.

The first night, I went with my mom and I didn't really like it. I thought, I don't need this program. I know what I did. I know it's wrong. I know better. But then I started going more often and I saw the program was giving me opportunities, like to work. I'd never had a job. I was only fifteen and never imagined having a job before I was eighteen.

But then Miss Colleen mentioned something about the food truck, which was just about to start. That interested me. I always behaved, but eventually I started participating in the program and when she gave me the opportunity to work on the truck, I really started liking the program. I saw there were mentors from UM, and all sorts of people there trying to help.

I started working and getting paid. With that money I was able to support my mom, considering the fact that she's a single parent and she has five kids, three who live with her, including myself. I'm the oldest at home. I have two younger brothers and two older brothers. I've been working on the truck for three years now, supporting my family.

I've gained a lot from the program. Besides work, the program follows a curriculum. Monday, Wednesday, and Saturday are regular program nights. We talk about issues in the city, behavior issues and how to control them, and plenty more. There's a special class on Thursday, which is an entrepreneur class, where we learn business skills, like how to make a résumé or a business plan.

On Saturdays we go to UM for tutoring and it helps a lot. Last quarter I had a D in math but with the help of the tutors, I have an A now.

The program has a different class on Monday for the guys on the food truck and those interested in working on the truck.

It's a Chef Class where we're trained by a personal chef and that's where I got most of my training.

I've had great experiences in the program. I'd never even been out of Miami before, but I went to Los Angeles with Miss Colleen, Mr. Jerry, and three other boys. We represented the Empowered Youth program at Homeboy Industries, which is a program similar to ours. I was on the stage and gave a speech about my experience in our program to about a hundred people. I never saw myself talking in front of people before.

Next was a really cool opportunity to go to Washington, D.C., sponsored by Commissioner Sarnoff. As part of the application, I had to write an essay, so I chose to write about my life and how it changed with Empowered Youth. Based on my essay and my good grades, I was chosen for the trip. It was amazing. I never experienced anything like that before. I was never into politics, but when I went to Washington, I got a lot of information and saw a lot of historic sites.

I got to go to a meeting at the White House with a man who has a program similar to ours [My Brother's Keeper]. Four boys from Empowered Youth represented our program and we talked about ways of working together.

After Washington, I applied for another opportunity to go to Costa Rica. My essay and application were selected and I went with another group of about fifteen kids from different high schools in Miami. I was the only representative from Empowered Youth on that trip.

That experience was amazing and it was my favorite trip so far. I got a chance to help out some kids who are unfortunate. They have a school, but it wasn't really nice compared to Miami-Dade County public schools. It was dirty and needed painting. It was missing some tables and chairs.

We made tables out of cement and tires and we made some chairs. We painted the walls and did some art on the walls.

They didn't really know English, so we kind of connected by them teaching us a little Spanish and we taught them some English.

While we were there, we went to the beach and stayed in an amazing mansion. I had a chance to meet new friends from Miami and Costa Rica and we still keep in contact through Facebook. It was fun to see their culture.

This program means a lot to me. Besides the crime issue that brought me here, I wasn't really thinking about college or where I'd be in the future. But going to these classes has taught me things, so now I'm prepared for my future. College is my next step.

For now, I want to stay in Florida, so I'm applying to UM, FSU, and FIU. The mentors from UM have worked with me to look at different colleges. They've shown me details like tuition costs and what percentage of students graduate from each college. I'm going to apply for financial aid and scholarships. I'm not sure what my major will be, but my idea is something culinary, since I've already started on it with the Empowered Youth program.

I've had a résumé since I was sixteen, although I haven't used it to apply for jobs since I've been working on the food truck. In the future, I hope to be able to work at the restaurant Miss Colleen is opening. Maybe someday I will be able to work up to a management job.

I would like for my future to be successful. Not rich, but enough to maintain and support myself and hopefully a family someday.

My older brothers are cool with me being in the program. They see it as a big life-changing opportunity and a great thing for me. I'm now trying to use my experience in the program to set an example for my younger brothers. My mom is proud and she brags about me. She tells everyone, "I have a son who went to the White House."

This program really works. It helps a lot of kids. Society sees these at-risk youth and believes their minds are rigged with crime and how they live in a war-zone and stuff. But inside is a whole different person. These kids don't have running water, they don't have lights; they only live with their mom and their dad is in jail. They have no resources. This program helps because it gives kids resources by giving them a chance to work and help them support their family, like what I'm still doing.

Miss Colleen is an angel. She and Mr. Jerry are like a second family. My mission for life was blurry at age fifteen, but now I see with tunnel vision. I can see my life step by step and I know what to do.

CHAPTER 16

One of the benefits of having my foot in the door of the juvenile justice system was learning the perspective of professional insiders. As an outsider who broke into foreign territory, I wondered if my visions and aspirations aligned with that of the experts.

I pieced together the picture as it was seen from the other side of the bureaucratic desk—that is, from the eyes of the government, most notably from Carlos Martinez, chief public defender, and Marie Osborne, chief assistant public defender, juvenile division.

Carlos Martinez, Chief Public Defender, Miami-Dade County

Because there are so many pressing community issues the government faces, each one tends to get looked at as a snapshot rather than a full-length film, which tends to minimize the life of an inner-city youth. The situation, as a whole, is rarely analyzed to determine the root causes and potential solutions to curb future problems.

Further exacerbating the situation, people go about their jobs differently. It's just human nature. So some folks really care about the kids, but to others it's just a job.

Some determined people, like Colleen, give it their all. Despite not having any money, they'll cobble things together to try to help the kids. On the other end are professionals in the system, whether it be defense counsel, prosecutor, or judge, who are inclined to focus on the here and now. They do what they have to do to dispose of the case, to get that piece of paper off their desk. They don't even refer to a child or even a person. It's called "case disposition."

So, as a daily course of action, the only consideration is what the crime was and what the statute allows in terms of sentencing. If the child is found guilty or pleads guilty, what does the statute allow? So there's a tendency of not looking at the whole life of the person, since oftentimes the only picture that's seen by the professionals in criminal justice is the crime. But not always. There are many profound exceptions in the juvenile and adult systems—professionals who factor in circumstances and will give people a second chance.

In recent years, the lowest-level offenders were thankfully diverted out of the juvenile justice system. First-time, second-time, and misdemeanor offenders are now better off because, most times, once children start down the path of the justice system, it screws them up even more.

Jailing youthful offenders is almost akin to complete failure because the system is ill-equipped to deal with the challenges of each child. Some of them are lifelong. Many of these children hail from a multigeneration history with the criminal court system. Efforts to break these two- and three-generation cycles become exceedingly difficult if deliberate intervention, support, and resources aren't provided.

The SEED Foundation[13] in Miami, D.C., and Maryland, provides a college-prep boarding school for underserved youth. This is one rare opportunity to remove the child from his current environment and place him into one with positive influences. So there are some points of intervention that are possible, and those need to be expanded, reinforced, and funded. Penal intervention or prison can make the situation worse, because the focus tends

---

[13] "About Our Model," The Seed Foundation, www.seedfoundation.com/about (accessed 3/15/17).

to be more disciplinary than rehabilitative, particularly in the adult system.

Once the youth outgrow the juvenile justice system, they enter the increasingly more punitive criminal justice system. Here, people involved even at the misdemeanor level get relegated to the criminal track, making them less employable once they have a record. These folks are forced into an underground economy and that becomes perpetual generational poverty and joblessness.

There's no simple solution, other than peeling back the layers of the onion to find the core problem. Some feel we have criminalized too many things. Some offenses could be handled as a civil offense, similar to code enforcement, rather than stigmatizing someone with a criminal record, arresting them, and getting them on that trajectory.

As a whole, our society has become decidedly punishment-oriented with the belief that the current methods will curb criminal behavior. In fact, the exact opposite is true. The existing solutions ingrain the behaviors even more, compounding the problems for already severely challenged communities.

Add to that the natural difficulties children have. Kids, by nature, do foolish things, without regard to the impact and consequences. Their natural behavior, particularly of teen boys, is to prove themselves by pushing limits and accepting challenges. Maybe it's a dare to steal a car. Or to bring a gun to school without getting caught. But when that kid gets caught with a firearm, he's kicked out of school and his trouble becomes a cumulative impact of all these things. Dares become more dangerous and costly in inner-city communities.

Another piece of the problem is that many inner-city youth don't get proper instruction and aren't seeing responsible behavior to model. If a person doesn't see a positive behavior, he can't emulate it. If the only behavior children see is negative, that's what they emulate.

The most effective corrective measures for this societal woe are rehabilitative programs that change people's thoughts, actions, and activities. However, these programs sorely lack precious funding, which is typically granted to the punishment-oriented programs instead.

Miami-Dade County has increased focus on getting wayward youth into counseling and other rehabilitative programs, but they can't handle the volume without state and federal resources, which aren't forthcoming.

Empowered Youth offers a positive alternative to this pressing conundrum, but a lasting solution requires an investment over time. It's an enormous challenge to turn this predicament around, but it's proven that mentoring works. It's especially successful when people learn job skills. The entrepreneurial skills the Empowered Youth boys learn allow them to start their own business without worrying about passing a background check.

From a purely political standpoint, the plight of inner-city youth falls into a black hole. Conservatives want to limit government spending and liberals push for more rehabilitative programs. But no one's actually looking at the community-wide issues as a whole. It's not that decision-makers don't want to fix the problems or don't believe diversion programs can address the issues, but the topic comes up short on the priority list.

CHAPTER 17

Now I knew that government officials like Carlos Martinez believed wholeheartedly in a program like mine, but couldn't help me financially. In fact, they saw every barrier stacked against me. His positive reinforcement fortifies my resolve and fuels my desire to strengthen the network surrounding my youth.

I've seen sincere connections develop repeatedly for anyone who's taken the time to get to know the boys. Empowered Youth becomes an invaluable extended family to the kids, who really need people who care about them.

I don't think there's ever been a tutor or mentor who doesn't say they got as much out of the program as the boys do. One UM student expressed the guilt she feels because she thinks she gets more out of it than she gives.

In the words of another student:

"I saw how wonderful it could be to simply share some of my time and skills with some of these young individuals that need extra help. I provided them with academic help they needed as well as a listening ear; I was able to build trust with them and encourage them to dream about their future and make plans, especially Mario; a fifteen-year-old boy who lost his dad a few years ago due to drug addiction. In return, they opened my eyes to deeper problems in the community, and encouraged me to strive for dreams to help the community once I graduate from college."

And another described her experience:

"During the semester, I was given the opportunity to work with a special group of kids at the Empowered Youth Program in the Liberty City community. The short time I spent with the young adults at the center deeply touched me and was an experience I won't forget."

Beyond the magic of the human connections is the educational piece; the tutoring program exposed my boys to the college atmosphere and college curriculum.

To most of my kids, college is as foreign as Siberia. Many students in the inner city don't graduate from high school, which reinforces the drop-out mentality for the younger children. Beyond that, college is a luxury that can't be fathomed by a person who doesn't have even his basic needs met.

So the exposure of my boys to the college environment opened a potential window to their future. As always, I capitalize on every opportunity available. As one example, the boys participate in the recruitment process for new student mentors. Presenting a brief speech to the classroom hones public speaking and marketing skills for the boys while offering the college students a glimpse of the youth they might be helping.

An example presentation to the class goes something like this:

"Hi, I'm Colleen Adams, executive director of Empowered Youth," I tell them. "I'm here to represent the mentorship program. Juan is a graduate of our program and he's going to tell you all about it."

As a seasoned veteran, Juan steps into action.

"Hello, everyone. My name is Juan and I'm here to talk about our program and see if you guys can help out and become mentors. Basically, I'm with Empowered Youth and I've been with the program for three years now. Empowered Youth is a program that deals with kids that are at-risk in the inner city. By 'at-risk' I mean kids that have been in the juvenile system and because of that we . . . they get sent to this program which is Empowered Youth. We help them by giving them resources they can't get in the inner city.

"Mentorship plays a big part. For myself, last semester, I had a special mentor. Her name is Brianna and she helped me study for the SAT and ACT. We also had a business competition and she helped me out with that. We had to make our own business plan—it was kind of like the *Shark Tank* idea.

"When you have a mentor, if you have an issue, they can help you solve it and talk about it, because at home sometimes we don't have that person to talk to. For myself, I live at home with my mom, so I don't have a father figure. I'm like the man of the house. I have three younger brothers. So when I get a mentor here, I get to talk about things. You guys play a very big role. Some way, somehow, you just make a difference."

I step back in.

"Juan is modest. He won't tell you that his grade point average went up from a 1.9 to a 2.5 now. He's going to college. Things that you take for granted in your lives, they are so spectacular to these boys—they are things that these boys just don't get. You have so much value to offer them. Working with inner-city kids who really don't have the same kind of opportunities that you probably do is really hands-on."

When we're fortunate to have a student in the class who's worked with us before, sometimes they sweeten the pitch even more.

One such young lady stepped up to address her classmates. "Working with Empowered Youth was one of the most rewarding experiences I've had at the University of Miami. You go there and you meet some extraordinary boys, like Juan and Chris and many others, and they're really cool. You'll hear their stories. You help them out with things like public speaking skills and their résumé. You help them out by teaching them things that the University teaches you and it's a great experience."

Sometimes the boys I bring to help me recruit are welcomed to join the remainder of the class and I'm always pleased when they accept. Their eagerness to learn and willingness to grab opportunities makes me hopeful that the same hunger will flow into their everyday lives.

The rewards of the mentorship program are beyond measure. There's a shiny nugget of gold awaiting anyone who gets involved.

CHAPTER 18

Every mentor contributes something valuable to the boys, but perhaps those who can offer the most hope are those who have walked through similar circumstances and not only survived, but thrived. Christopher is one example.

Christopher, Mentor

Prior to becoming an attorney, I was a banker. But even before that, I grew up in a similar situation as did the Empowered Youth guys and I faced many of the same obstacles they face: absent parents, locked-up father, and so on. I got in trouble when I was younger, spent time in a diversion program, and I got my record expunged. I was also in a drug program. But by the grace of God, I've overcome many of those challenges.

I've always loved community service and volunteering, but the interactive format with Empowered Youth is the most special to me because it's very cathartic. Most people don't spend the time to just sit and reflect or talk with themselves. When you come from an inner-city environment and you don't have positive role models, you're not taught self-reflection. Instead, you're probably taught the opposite.

Many times when I'm talking to the boys, I feel like I'm having a conversation I still need to have with myself, since I still have a lot of unresolved feelings. When I'm talking to them it's not like I'm speaking *at* them, it's a conversation between us, even if they're not responding. Even if it's just their body language.

I know it's important for them to have someone they can relate to. Sometimes I can provide that, and sometimes maybe not. In some cases I'm too far removed from the situation, from either a generational or socio-economic standpoint. But I think it's necessary that they see someone who's been there and gotten beyond it. It really makes a difference.

I went to law school with David [another mentor] and we became friends when we were on a trial team together. I was new to the Miami area and was trying to find ways to get involved. David told me about his work at Empowered Youth, which was right up my alley since I love working with at-risk youth. I've been coming to the program for a few years, as often as I can, based on what's happening in my life.

Sometimes the boys need a one-on-one conversation outside of a huge circle of thirty people. That's why the smaller group breakout sessions are so helpful.

One kid, Juan, reminds me of myself. He's a good kid. He wasn't around the best role models and found himself in trouble. If you were to look at his rap sheet, many people would develop a picture of someone whom he's not. It's wonderful to see the work he puts in to improve his life. He's graduated from the program and his record is expunged. I know he won't be in trouble again.

You hear about the rate of recidivism for troubled youth and the reason why it's so high is that people have to return to their insidious environments. So I enjoy seeing the man Juan is becoming. And I don't take credit. If anything, I give credit to Miss Colleen. This program survives because of her. Empowered Youth is meeting a need that's not being met in other ways.

Juan is a shining example. He makes everything worth it. I always say that even if it's just one person you save, it was worth it. If it's one at a time, eventually those numbers will add up. Then those successful young men will go back to their communities and become an example for others. One of the biggest things we need is for the people who "make it" to come back and show the others what's possible.

Studies have shown that the trauma experienced by these kids when they see many of their loved ones killed in inner-city violence is the same trauma experienced by inhabitants of war-torn countries, but our youth are not given the same attention. There's a human side of this. We can't forget these are children at the end of the day.

CHAPTER 19

Hakim,[14] EY Student

I'm in the tenth grade now, but when I was younger, I felt like I was too old for my original group of friends—like they were too immature. They would walk around and throw eggs and other childish stuff. So I started slowly moving on and gravitated to another group.

School was horrible. I hated going and I skipped a lot. I was kind of a delinquent. I was the one who would walk into a store and mess stuff up. I'd be the type to spray a stinky scent near a customer. Over the years my actions got bigger and bigger.

About three months ago, I made a mistake with one of my friends and got charged with grand theft, trespassing, and burglary. Two of those charges got dropped and we came to an agreement with the judge on the last charge. The agreement was that if I go to the Empowered Youth program, to help change me for the better, they would seal my record.

When I first came, I felt shy. I felt different. At first, I didn't realize the program was for kids who had offended, so I thought I was the only one in my situation. I thought it was just another therapy program.

I'll be honest, my first couple of weeks, I thought the program was a joke. But getting a month or so into it, I started realizing that the activities I thought were just picked out randomly, were actually making changes in me, for the better. Like my attitude. It was horrible back then. I was antisocial. I had an attitude with everyone and anyone.

---

[14] Name has been changed to protect the privacy of the family.

One thing that made a difference for me was all the activities where I was forced to talk. The first thing that happens when we get to the program is Mr. Calvin, our youth instructor, he will ask us about our day or how our week is going. He always asks. Sometimes people aren't used to talking, but they start talking about their day and that's kind of how I stopped being antisocial. A lot was happening at school, so I started talking more about it.

The activities help improve communication skills and that also helped me overcome being antisocial. It always seems like they start as random activities, but they end up teaching me something.

In one activity, we were given a card that had different topics listed on it. We had to find a partner, one we'd never talked to before, and we had to describe what was on the card. He kind of tricked us, but in a good way. He said, "You guys have two rounds, two minutes in each round."

In the first two minutes, we talked for about thirty seconds. During the second two minutes, we got used to talking to each other and we talked for about four minutes. The instructor knew we ran over time, but he didn't want to stop the clock. He kept it going and stopped us after a while.

Ever since then, I've noticed improvement in my communication skills. I'm more comfortable talking to people now.

The Saturday tutoring classes at UM also helped me in a big way. Plus, we get pizza! They cover all types of subjects. I can bring my homework on any topic and they will help me. The tutors show me things I never knew. I only take geometry, because I feel that's what I'm best at and I want to learn more so I can keep going on to honors classes. After just a couple of weeks in the program, I passed almost all my math tests with an A. I was always studying two or three lessons ahead of the class and I was one of the fastest workers. I'm also happy to say that this whole sophomore year, I haven't skipped school at all. I've attended every single day, except the days I have to go to court.

Even before Empowered Youth, I've always been a cook and the program has shown me I want to stay in culinary. I've been cooking since I was about ten or eleven years old. I'm always around my mom in the kitchen and I watch her. I would cut carrots and anything else to help her. I slowly evolved to helping in all areas of the kitchen. I'd make my way to the pan, then the grill and oven.

One day I was in the car with Miss Colleen. I was talking about my family and how we were kind of stuck financially. She started talking about the job opportunity on the food truck, and she offered it to me a few different times. I kept declining. I didn't feel I could do it and also felt it would take too much time.

One night she was dropping me off at 79th Street so I could get picked up by my mother and she brought it up again. "Just remember, you're always welcome on the food truck," she said. That night, I changed my mind.

"You know what, Miss Colleen? I'll take the offer," I said.

As soon as I got out of the car, she got out and went to the trunk to get me a shirt and cap and she told me I'd start in a week.

My work on the food truck has taught me that it's not all so easy. I've gotten better in my knife skills and a lot better on the flattop. I learned how to use a fryer, like how to turn on the fryer without burning myself.

When we have a new recipe, Chef Chantelle or Chef Emmanuel will show us how to make it, either during chef class or while prepping prior to an event. Two of the new things we had at our last event were a veggie wrap and chicken fingers. The chicken fingers weren't so hard. We just dipped them in flour before frying them.

I work every weekend now. My family consists of me and my mom, an older sister, older brother, and a younger brother. We aren't all that wealthy, so every paycheck I get goes straight to the family and whatever's left, I take it.

Ever since I've been in the program, I've been helping my mother around the house. She and I get along a lot more now. My mom's sick a lot since she suffers from migraines, so whenever she can't cook, I do.

I'm a mentor to my younger brother a lot more than I used to be. My older brother doesn't get along with the others in the house. He's always picking on or bothering my sister. My little brother tries to follow his footsteps by hitting or scaring my sister. I will stop him from doing that. If he gets too physical, I'll grab him and pull him away, but if he doesn't touch her, I'll just be like "Yo! Get outta her face! Stop being a dick!"

I've cut off a whole list of my old friends: the drug dealers, pot smokers, and pretty much all the bad influences. I just became friends again with one of my best friends who I lost a while ago. I started playing basketball a lot more with the kids I used to hang with when I wasn't such a bad kid.

I have three or four months left of the Empowered Youth program. After we graduate, we have an option to stay as a mentor, or visit once in a while to talk to the new kids about our experience. We've had plenty of guest speakers since I've been in the program and they're all inspiring, so my plan is to come back to talk to the newer kids once I graduate.

Empowered Youth is one of the best second chances I've ever gotten and I plan to finish my work in the food truck. We take culinary classes every Monday night for eight months, and then I'll get a certificate. Once I have that, I'll apply at major restaurants, such as Joe's Stone Crab or The Crab House.

Before I came to Empowered Youth, I'd never heard of it. I knew there were programs, but I never knew they were this great. I've been to one other program before. It was like single-kid therapy, and it was nothing like this. It was boring. This is so different. You get used to it and then you start getting more comfortable with it.

The first night I came, they had some pizza. I wanted a slice of that pizza so badly, but I was so shy that I never got up. Then the box ran out. But now, as soon as we get to the program, everyone crowds around the table. We help set up everything, then we all dig in.

Since my first days, I've made a lot of friends in the program. Sadly one of them just reoffended, but that happens, I guess. My old group of friends are cool with me moving on.

I don't let little things get to me anymore. That's another change from the program. It was a slow development, but everything came together.

I'm happy to say I'm in Empowered Youth now. I've changed for the better and I'm still in progress. This is the best second chance I ever had in my life and I plan to make good use of this opportunity. Honestly, if I wasn't in this program, I would probably be in the streets right now doing something so wrong.

Miss Colleen has been so wonderful to me ever since we met. She even gave me a hug that first day. She'll ask me how I am because she's caring. I've never had someone other than a family member be that caring. She's become a second mom.

CHAPTER 20

Working on the food truck provides invaluable business experience for youth like Hakim, but even more priceless is the relationship the boys develop with the training chefs. Many well-meaning people come and go, flowing in and slipping out like the tide, but Chef Emmanuel is a rock-solid, loyal keeper. I can always count on him doing whatever he does in the best possible way. He's wonderful with the kids and a terrific role model. His engaging rapport with customers is a valuable and necessary example for the boys.

Our chef's position is unique. They deal with young men who lack training and experience, and whose challenging attitude is a survival mechanism. They've seen that nice people become victims in the hood.

Emmanuel understands. He's able to bring out the best in the boys as well as de-escalate rising tension. His role extends far beyond a culinary job.

Other chefs without an inner city background have had greater difficulty dealing with the kids. It's hard for most people to understand that at the heart of a poor attitude is really just someone who's been hurt a lot. But when a person understands how to work with our youth, the relationship becomes pivotal.

Chef Emmanuel

Growing up was rough for me, being raised by a single mom. I'm the oldest of four boys and we had no father around.

I always knew I wanted to cook and I got started at P.F. Chang's restaurant. When I left there, my friend gave me a chance at Joe's Stone Crab. When I told them I was a cook, they said that didn't matter, that you have to start from the bottom in the restaurant business.

They put me in the back prep area doing simple stuff like spinach and soup. From there they moved me to the cook line, the fry station and sauté fry. I moved up to salad then sauté. Then grill to broiler. Finally flattop.

My bosses said that because I was doing really well and mastered the whole line, they wanted me to do employee feeding. That's a hard job. When you feed all the employees in the restaurant, you have to worry about food cost, how many people you're feeding, how many pounds of rice will feed a certain number of people, portion control, and saving some for night shift. I have the help of three guys who took me under their wings.

Through another chef, I met Sharie, who told me Miss Colleen was building this program for juvenile kids to give them a second chance. I came to check it out and I stayed. Since I've been working with the boys, we've been through a lot. I taught them how to cook and prep. Every experience I got from Joe's, I brought it right back to teach these guys.

We have three sections in the truck, the flattop and fryer area, the prep area, and the window. If I know my window person is really good, I will rotate him and put somebody new in the window and try to teach him. Sometimes they get frustrated, because they're young. Once I get them to the window and they experience it, then they get used to it.

When I see they get used to it, I switch it around and put someone else out there. Some are not good spellers, but I encourage them. We're not all great spellers, but we have to try while writing the tickets. I promise you, these kids are willing to learn.

When we bring in something new, we have to start teaching them from pre-K and all the way up. They have to know every last thing about it, like the measurements and the ounces of the ingredients.

During their training, we teach them how to make things like pasta. We did fried chicken wings, and I showed them it's better with more seasoning. We also did blackened tilapia. I taught them how to use a sauté pan, make mac and cheese, turkey burgers, lobster rolls, and lamb. At events, we did mango salsa salad.

Sometimes they say they want to try some new stuff. I'll say, "Alright, bring something to me. We'll make it. If we like it, we'll serve it."

It's also about presentation and how to make everything pretty. We're hands-on. We show them, then they can take it wherever they want to go.

The kids who really come to learn make me happy. For example, Hercules—the little one, the rude one. And then Stanley, he's young. He makes me happy when I see him, because this fourteen-year-old kid wants to work! Six, seven, or eight hours per day, making $100. That money will keep him off the street. I'm glad he's willing to work, because not everybody is.

My other guy is Juan. Even when he has girlfriend problems, he makes me laugh. He's like another brother. He's been with the program as long as I have. I know his whole family and he's been through a lot of situations. When the truck was at Wynwood Yard, Juan did the prep that he learned just by watching us and then he started orchestrating the group—telling this guy to do this, and that guy to do that, and everything went perfectly. That excited me, because someone who didn't go to culinary art school just took what we showed him and ran with it.

Another kid, Hakim. I like this kid because when he gets to the window he gets pissed off and he really wants to blow.

"Get me off this window, Chef. They're getting me so mad," he'll say.

"Chill, just relax," I tell him. At that point I would take the window and try to make the people happy, by giving them free stuff or whatever it takes.

There's the goofy kid, Vernon. One day I got him mad and he said, "I didn't like what you said."

"What? Alright, I'm sorry," I said and then we got right back to being silly again.

Then there are people who think they know more than everybody, but they don't know anything. Like Reggie. He never wanted to be at the window because he has anger problems and no people skills. Once I told him, "Listen, you have to deal with it regardless, because this is your money and your life. You have to talk to people." Now he has no problem being in the window. He does it perfectly and talks to people. He's a hard nut, but a funny comedian, too.

I got soft guys, I got tough guys. I got gangster kids. I got it all. They teach me new hood words every day that I never knew in my life.

I know how to get the boys mad and how not to get them mad. They get mad real fast. Every last one of those kids tests you. But in building a relationship with them, I don't take them as their mentor, because it's closer than that. I take them as my brothers. We've been doing this and growing together.

One of the boys has a family with like six or seven kids in the house and they're sharing everything and there just isn't money. So by working, they can buy things on their own. That makes them really happy. If they want ice cream, they don't have to ask their parents.

Every one of these kids needs a mentor. There are two types of people influencing them. The bad ones say, "Let's go do this or that" to get money, and then the good ones, like Miss

Colleen, say, "Alright, let me take you on the right path. I'll take you to work with me and teach you something you don't know so you can learn, then run with it in the future."

I think about how we can keep this program going because, without Miss Colleen or Mr. Jerry or me, who's going to help them? This business can grow. These kids are willing to listen. "If you aren't willing to listen, I don't need you," I tell them. Once I tell them I don't need them and they see that I mean it, that's when they ask for a second chance. Half of them did start over with another chance.

They're working for something and learning a lot. Business skills and chef and culinary classes, and everything is hands-on. I'm teaching half of these guys how to speak with people, because not everyone knows how.

When a customer hears "Yo" or "Wha's up, fool?" they don't like that. It's not like we're in the Bronx or the ghetto. These are like real-life people in front of you. You would never normally see them or they would look right past you. They would never say "Hi" to you. You have to learn how to jump in their circle. That's how life is. If you can't jump into that circle, how're you going to succeed?

I had to learn it the hard way. I saw the kids trying to talk to people and the people looked away, like, "I don't need your flyer." But if you get on their level, they respond. I teach these kids to say, "Hey, how're you doing? My name is Fred." I tell them how to interact with the customers and they've learned that when they're friendly, the customers interact back. Business has been growing because I've been teaching them how to speak with people.

It's really hard in the hood, so they appreciate when someone is willing to help them. I find ways to help, but sometimes I have to take a problem to Miss Colleen and we find a solution together. With multiple kids, we have multiple problems. She finds a solution to help every last one of them. When they have nothing, she helps. When they have babies, she helps. The kids don't have Christmas, so she makes it happen.

I'm young myself, so I'm a friend to them. I'll tell them what they need to hear, even if it's a tough call, like, "That will end you up in jail." I'm a family member who's trying to steer them in the right direction, like a big brother.

For some of these guys, their only home is at their job. That's why they're willing to wake up at 6 a.m. for work. That's dedication. Half of them used to be late, but Miss Colleen tells them, "I don't need you if you're late," and they turn it around. She makes it happen.

The biggest challenges are that some of them don't want to let people in because they don't know the outcome. But once they get comfortable, they open up. They have a lot of trust issues because they've been turned on multiple times.

The mentors in the program come from far away just to see these kids. These volunteers have their own family and their own businesses. We have pastors and people who could be doing whatever they want to do, but they choose to come sit next to these boys in the circle group to show them love. Now that's a lot of love that you don't normally get in life.

Some of the boys take it and run with it. Some appreciate it, some I don't know. Some take the skills with them, some don't. But we try no matter what.

I'm there for these kids 100 percent. When they need something, they have a group at Empowered Youth who will do anything for them. Sometimes they don't get it. Maybe they don't get it today, and maybe not even tomorrow, but down the line, they see it and say, "I see what you were talking about."

There's a lot going on with this program and I appreciate what Miss Colleen's doing, because when I was a child, I didn't get this kind of help. Even though I didn't grow up with everything, I see why now, because sometimes it's good not to grow up with everything. You appreciate why later.

Miss Colleen deserves a trophy for what she does, and she does a lot. You don't know why she does it. She wakes up every day and works, works, works. She doesn't sleep, she's always tired. It's a big headache. But I see the respect the kids have for her. Many people wouldn't have kids returning to them like she does. When boys who graduated from the program are still referring to her as their mother and keeping in touch, that's total respect.

Mr. Jerry's another father to the business. He makes it happen when we have problems with the food truck. He helps make all this possible.

You can tell when you've met somebody whom you appreciate. These are the people I appreciate. They make a living for these kids, they make a living for me and they make a living for everybody around us. These are the best people I ever met in my life.

CHAPTER 21

Emmanuel isn't our only chef who relates well to the boys and who's committed to educating them in culinary skills as well as the culinary profession. In the Trinity Cathedral kitchen, Chef Ali plunged into his first class with the boys to assess their current skill level. As the students chimed in randomly, the conversation ricocheted around the room like an enchanted boomerang.

Chef Class

"Let's make sure we have what we need, like cutting boards. Do you all know the difference between the different colors? Who can tell me?" asks the chef.

"Raw meat is red. Produce is green. Lettuce is white?" a student guesses.

"Red is for meat: steaks, ground meat, veal, lamb. What about yellow? . . .Yellow is for chicken and chicken only. You don't cut anything but chicken on yellow. Because chicken has to be cooked at a certain temperature. We have to cook it to 165 degrees. If it's not, it makes you sick, especially kids. So when you cook your chicken, I would prep it on a completely different side. I wouldn't even put it on the table with anything else. I don't want chicken up against anything but chicken itself.

"Beef, red meat, or lamb can be cooked to 155 degrees or even lower. That's why steaks can be cooked less, at like medium-rare or rare. It can be cooked at different temperatures, unlike chicken that has to be cooked to 165 degrees at all times. Same thing for turkey and anything poultry-like.

"The blue board is for seafood. Fish, lobster, shrimp. You can prep seafood and meat on the same table, but make sure you keep them separate so they don't cross-contaminate. I'm going to teach you how to not cross-contaminate and still keep things really efficient in the kitchen.

"Fruit and vegetables use the white board."

"One thing we need that I don't see here is sanitation buckets for cleaning. There's a red one and there's a green one. Do you have them on the truck?"

"Yes."

"We need to have them in here [training kitchen], too."

"Do you know the difference between the color buckets?"

"Yeah."

"You tell me."

"I think the red one is for meat, right?" a student asks.

"No, the red one is for sanitizing. The green one is for soap and water. For sanitizing, you can just wipe a spot. Okay, where do you bring the food truck?"

"To all sorts of venues," one student responds.

"I'm going to develop a menu besides burgers and fries and I'll come and check you out on the truck. I haven't seen it yet, but usually the quarters are tight. I'll assist you and show you how to move around."

"Oh, it's tight," one guy admits and they all chuckle.

"Have you worked with knives yet?"

"Yeah, we worked with knives."

"We're going to need a few more cutting boards. I want you to practice your cutting skills. If you don't have textbooks, I'll bring some of my own and bring some photocopies so you can see different cutting techniques and different terminology. How about cutting an onion?"

"Yeah."

"Properly? Like what's the proper way?"

The crowd mumbles.

"Not everyone cuts the right way, so we're going to practice that. What have y'all cooked other than burgers and hotdogs?"

"A lot of stuff. Macaroni, Reubens. We make everything."

"Mac and cheese. Potato salad," offers another student.

"Y'all really cooking for real!"

"Oh yeah!"

"We're getting our certification..." someone answers.

"Yes, that's another thing. We're going to work to get your certification in sanitation. That's going to be very important, because once you have that, you can pretty much work in any kitchen. The certification usually lasts about five years. You have to take a test to renew it. You definitely need that. If inspectors come and not everyone has their license they can shut the whole truck down. They will ask you about food safety and temperatures for different meats—like what we just talked about.

"Also how to store things in the fridge. For example, if we had a bunch of meat in this fridge right now, where would you put the chicken?"

"On the bottom," several said at once.

"Exactly. Because if anything from another meat falls on the chicken, it will be okay because chicken has to be cooked hotter than anything else. But if you put chicken at the top and the steaks at the bottom, and the chicken drips onto the steak and someone wants a medium-rare, they can get salmonella poisoning. So we definitely need to be careful about that. So chicken is always at the bottom, then you have your red meat, then seafood, then if you have enough space, you would put your greens and fruits all the way at the top. But normally I would keep that separate. If there were two different fridges, I would put fruits and veggies in one and meat in another, so everything is separate and no chance for cross-contamination. So, what do y'all want to learn?"

"Desserts."

"What kind of desserts?" the chef asks.

"Cheesecake."

"Oreo."

"A donut."

"Luther burger!"[15]

"Called a who?" asks the chef.

"A Luther burger. With donuts!"

"Lunar?" The chef hasn't heard of it.

"Luther."

"That would be the number one sandwich right there!" one student exclaims.

"How much is that sandwich?" they ask their new mentor.

"Cost it out. You have to think about how much you can charge for it and how much it is for you to make it. You have to start thinking about your profit margin. You have to think about the cost of the ground beef and how many patties you can make out of that. Do you use one donut and cut it in half or two donuts?"

"Two donuts."

"You need to press the donuts. Do you have a press on the truck?"

"How much would you charge for it?" one student inquires.

"With bacon on it?" another student suggests.

---

[15] The Luther Burger is a bacon cheeseburger with grilled Krispy Kreme doughnuts in place of buns. It's rumored to be named after singer Luther Vandross, who is rumored to be its creator. See http://burgerbeast.com/2010/03/26/krispy-kreme-doughnut-burger-aka-luther-burger-at-miami-dade-county-fair (accessed 12/9/16).

"Well, how many ounces of meat would we use for each burger? Four ounces. I would say ten dollars. Do y'all do combo burger with fries?" the chef asks the class.

"Yeah."

"So you would do a Luther burger with fries for twelve dollars," the chef replies.

The room explodes with excited chattering, almost like their team who'd been trailing had just pulled into the lead. Except it was over a hamburger.

"So with that type of burger, are you going to put lettuce and tomato?" a student asks.

"No. I mean, you can. That's something you would ask. I wouldn't want it, but some people might, so you want to give them the option. You would ask when you take the order. Bacon would also be optional and an extra dollar.

"I'll show you how to flip things in the pan. I think everyone here should know how to do that."

"I tried and was spilling stuff all out of the pan," one student admits.

"That way you don't always have to have a spoon handy. You can just swish - and keep it going. You can't be slow and scared when you do it. You can't do it with too much liquid in the pan or it will splatter. So, grits? Who makes grits?"

"My grits come out haaaard."

"You need to start thinking about replacing water in your cooking, since there's no flavor in it. You have to season it up, so I would start using some stock or chicken broth."

"Chicken pull?"

"No, chicken broth."

"What that do?"

"You eat turkey, right?"

"Yeah."

"Afterward you take what's left and boil it up in water with some onions and celery, salt, pepper, then boil it down for hours and all the flavors will blend into the water, making a broth. Then you can use that flavorful liquid to make your rice or other sauces and it enhances the flavor. I'll show you how to make that. You can do the same thing with beef bones.

"You can also use the broth in grits."

"In grits?"

"Anywhere you use water in cooking.

"You also need to think about colors. Think of your plate as your canvas. As you're putting a plate together, think about the colors. If it looks too green, what can you add to it? Something red. What's red? Tomatoes, red peppers, chili peppers."

• • •

From cutting boards and salmonella to Luther burgers and colors on a plate. To observe a classroom full of inner-city boys thoroughly engaged in a conversation about food is to witness a real-life fairy tale.

CHAPTER 22

Chef Ali jumped feet-first into the technical aspect of cooking, but soon after, the session turned personal.

Chef Class

"Where do you work?" the students asked their new mentor.

"In private homes. I originally wanted to be a restaurant manager. That may be for you or maybe not for you. As I got into a restaurant, I started to realize it meant doing the same thing over and over and over again. And then a friend of mine was throwing a Fourth of July pool party for three hundred people and she asked, 'Do you want to cook for me? I first thought, that's crazy. But then I thought, You know what? I'm going to make my own food and I'm going to do this.

"So I created a menu. Chicken wings, burgers and dogs, salads, fruit. My friend and I did the whole thing ourselves. And afterwards, I realized there was more to being a chef than working in a restaurant. You could provide a service in people's homes.

"In a restaurant you might work fourteen hour shifts and make ten or twelve dollars per hour, which is cool when you're starting out. I would suggest if you want to be a chef you have to work in a restaurant first because if you don't, you won't learn how to run a kitchen. There are different rules and different ways to move around.

"After working in a restaurant for two years, I was doing my own catering thing on the side. I decided I wanted my own company. My first client was a huge fraternity at the University of Miami. About twenty kids live there and they have their own chef. As part of the interviewing process, I had to prepare a meal and explain why I should be the chosen chef. It was me against five other people.

"That was my first time stepping outside the restaurant. I knew my food was good, so I wasn't worried about that. I'd just never been in the position to have to tell people what to do, I was used to my restaurant manager telling *me* what to do. I got the job and the first week was horrible. I'm not going to lie and try to brag about it or say I was killing it. I had to buy food and was cooking for more people than I ever had before in a house environment. I had to make a budget. I had to pretty much learn a whole new routine because I was used to doing my little gig about once a month for events, but this was now every day. So I pretty much had to buy food for a week for twenty kids for breakfast, lunch, and dinner every Monday through Friday.

"So I had to wake up at five o'clock in the morning, figure out the menu, then buy the food. I usually shop for the week, but sometimes I shop for the day. I learned when you have twenty people you're cooking for, everybody's taste is different. So I created a menu that included two breakfast options, two lunch options, and one dinner option. I sent the choices in an e-mail and once I saw what most people wanted, that's what I'd make.

"That's one thing you'll learn, you have to control your costs. As soon as you start buying for just one meal, now you've got all this leftover product that will end up going bad, so you'd better figure out something else to do with it.

"I'm going to show you how to calculate costs. When you're shopping, you need to manage your budget. What can you buy for one hundred dollars or how you can make more with less? Sometimes you might get into a situation with your family where you have fifty dollars for groceries. What can you get for it? You'll get to a point where you will walk into a store and you've been there so much that you'll just know what chicken costs off the top of your head. And salmon. Peppers. Onions. Some people have to look up costs, but I know them. I'm in the grocery store at least two or three times a day."

Groans drift around the room.

"It's annoying to go to the store so often, but the more you do it, the less time you have to spend there. I don't spend more than twenty-five minutes in the store per day. I know exactly what I'm there for and what it's going to cost me. Unless there's a sale, then I load up on it. I'm going to take advantage of sales to help keep overall food costs down.

"So, anyway, I definitely suggest that if you like the food truck, then a restaurant would be a good next step. Maybe something small like a Chili's or Fridays. I wouldn't recommend fast food, only because you won't learn the same things you'll learn working in a real restaurant, like Chili's, Fridays, or even Cheesecake.

"Speaking of Cheesecake, I have a funny story. Before I decided to become a chef, my first job out of high school was at the Cheesecake Factory. That was the worst job ever because they're very serious. Like, I was just there for the money. My friend who worked there told me how much he was making and I thought it was the way to go.

"But once I got back there, people were cussing at me. When you're working in a real kitchen, there's no *nice*. Orders are coming in and people are all over and there's no time to hold your hand and be nice. And I didn't know that beforehand. My dad was a chef for years, but I never went to work with him to see how he worked and he never came home with that kind of vibe.

"So when I got to Cheesecake, I just wanted to make money, so I was pushing. I was a busboy and the chef was cussing and telling me to move my cart and I wasn't used to that. So I quit. And when I decided to go to culinary school a couple of years later, I kind of remembered that. Then, when the chef treated me the same way, I wasn't surprised and I just realized then that there was no room for nice.

"One of my favorite sayings was, 'There's no need to be nice in the kitchen. Just get the job done and go home.' Because when you get in the situation when it's a Friday night and tickets are coming through for fifty people, you've got to *move*.

"There's this thing called 'ticket time.' When you go to a restaurant and you don't get your food, you don't like that. Some people in the back of the house understand and they want to make sure the food is coming out, but there are others who don't care. You need to learn about ticket time.

"It's like on the food truck, if someone orders a burger. Most burgers, depending on how they want it cooked, take about nine minutes to get a medium-well burger out. People are willing to wait, but when it's going on fifteen or twenty minutes, people will be upset. So, remember, there's no room for nice.

"You may have a manager yelling at you, but don't take it personally. I finally realized that the people cussing at me were just trying to make sure things were moving fast. So, if you realize this, it will be an easier transition if you work in a restaurant."

"Do you yell at your staff?" a brave soul asked and drew a round of chuckles.

"Of course! It's not personal! I tell my lady right now, there's me at home and then there's me when I'm in the kitchen. I'm a whole different person. I don't have time for nice or any excuses. *No*. Just get out of the way.

"As a perfect example, I had a friend helping me out at a party for sixteen people. I'm cooking all the food. Three courses for sixteen people. By myself. My friend wanted to tag along to see how it goes, so I told her, 'Bring your big girl pants. These people are paying me a lot of money and I need to make sure they're getting the services they expect.'

"As a chef, that's going to frustrate you, but you always have to keep your composure, because customers are going to say things like, 'This isn't the right way.' Remember that the customer's always right."

Now he was speaking a language the boys knew.

"The other day on the food truck, this lady came up and we didn't have any straws and she was like, 'Really? You can't sell smoothies without a straw.' She was, like, all attitude...And I'm like, Damn," said one boy.

"That's right! That's going to happen. You know the phrase: The customer's always right. Stick that in your head, because that will keep you cool. There'll be people, especially when you're dealing face-to-face with a person, like on the food truck. You have to understand that somebody might be upset that something may not come out right. Just apologize and say, 'How can I fix it for you?' If you can, just take care of it. This is a job. Do your job. The customer's always right. Say, 'I apologize for the inconvenience.'"

Another boy chimes in. "Sometimes when it gets packed, like real packed, with a lot of people coming to the food truck, there will be somebody who comes and starts . . . 'I didn't get my food! Where's my food?'"

"That's what I'm saying! In a calm manner, just say, 'We'll take care of it. The orders are coming out. Please be patient with us.' People just want to be heard. They want to feel they're acknowledged when they complain about something. Listen and keep your cool.

"When I applied at T.G.I. Fridays, the manager asked about prior experience. I told him the Cheesecake Factory story and he laughed and then hired me. I told him I'd do whatever he needed me to do and he started me by sitting people down. For three months, I was pretty much in the front before I could even start taking orders. He basically made me learn the entire restaurant and I thank him for that, because sometimes people go straight to the kitchen. But when you understand the front *and* the back, you understand how to get food out quick. When you're in the front, you see how customers complain about certain things, so when you get to the back, you understand. You have to take pride in what you do.

"When my food comes out, it's beautiful. At all times. I don't want anybody coming back to me saying something was wrong. Some people don't take pride because to them it's just a paycheck, but for me, this was what I wanted to do. In any case, it's about the quality of your work. You don't want a certain burger with the cheese dripping off the side and the toast burnt, and you don't serve fries that are burnt to a crisp. That shows you don't care.

"It took me ten months before I got to the job that requires someone to know all the other aspects of the restaurant: the expediter at the ticket window. When I got in the kitchen, they put me on salads first; that's the easiest station in the kitchen. Two months later, I asked to work the fryer. Then sauté, then the grill. I spent time as a dishwasher. I wanted to know everything so anywhere I go, I could do any position.

"I take pride in food and if I'm the expediter and you give me Alfredo that looks like soup, I'm sending it back. The chefs will cuss at you for doing that, but the expediter's job is to make sure every plate goes out beautiful. Or somewhere close.

"Your experience working directly with the public on the food truck is great experience. If you're working the window and someone hands you a burger that doesn't look right, hand it back and say, 'Make this again,' because you don't want to serve that and have it come back on you."

"Chef Emmanuel always tells us not to serve something we wouldn't want to eat."

"There's nothing better than putting food in front of someone and they can't even talk because the food is so good.

"I was kind of nervous when I started cooking for Norris Cole,[16] because it was my first time cooking for a professional athlete in his home. I'm like, I gotta give him something that's over the top.

"I was there for three nights a week during the season, before he got traded.

"One day I told him I'm making tilapia with shrimp and stir-fried vegetables. A miso tilapia. I brought the plates in and served the food to him and his manager, and it just got really quiet. All I heard was the fork scraping against the plate. They loved every bite. And that's the feeling you want every time.

"It might be the simplest dish ever. It could be some regular mac and cheese. But you want the people eating it to think, This is the best mac and cheese I ever had. Or, this is the best hotdog, or the best burger.

"That's what I mean by working with pride. That's what I want you to walk away with, whether you're going to be a chef, an electrician, a firefighter, or whatever. You want to be the best you can be at whatever you choose for your future. When you're an artist and I pay you to paint a picture of me, but it doesn't end up looking like me, people will move on to the next person.

"You don't do anything half-assed. You'll start to be known for that and that will become your reputation.

"As part of the application for the UM fraternity job, we had to a make a dish. I wasn't going to make just one dish, because every chef applying would be making one dish. I decided to make a dessert, too.

---

[16] Former Miami Heat basketball player.

"The crazy part was I made a veggie Alfredo pasta and I served it up. He said, 'You put too much on my plate. I'm not going to eat all that, I'm not hungry.' But I still put it on and he started eating while we were talking and then he stopped talking for a second and I just heard the fork clicking. He said he wasn't hungry but he ate the whole thing. At that point I told him I had a dessert. 'Why'd you make a dessert?' he asked. 'I wanted to show you what I can do,' I told him. He ate the *whole* thing.

"No matter what job you have, you try to learn everything you can and then you're qualified to do more. Don't sit there and wait for an opportunity. If you see something, go for it."

. . .

Cooking, working, survival, and life skills are all intertwined in one dynamic package that engages every student. In the blink of an eye, more positive connections are ingrained and strangers are transformed into a posse with a common goal: food.

CHAPTER 23

Fernando,[17] EY Student

My family's originally from Honduras. My father was sixteen years old when my mother was pregnant with me. They had no money, so my dad decided to come to the United States to get a job and send money back to my mom. He attempted fourteen times to get to the United States before finally making it. He never quit. Once he got here, he found a job, became a chef, and sent money and clothes back to me and my mom.

Then he wanted to bring the rest of the family, but he couldn't bring two people at the same time because it was too expensive, so he brought my mom. They made money together while I stayed with my grandma in Honduras. Once they saved enough money, my mom paid for me and my dad paid for my grandma and we both came to the United States. Since then, they brought the whole extended family.

My trouble began with my anger, which I got from my dad. He had a temper since he was a boy and he liked to fight anyone who messed with him, to prove he was stronger. So I have those genes. My anger issues started leading me to trouble, but I was off doing my own thing, so my parents didn't really realize what was happening.

Anything people said to me ticked me off and I went into fight mode to solve the problem. I was having a lot of arguments. People were trying to get to me and I wouldn't let it go, even holding onto situations from years ago. I'd keep all that bad stuff in my head.

---

[17] Name has been changed to protect the privacy of the family.

Finally, I was getting so tired of it. I was having a whole bunch of arguments with different people so I felt like I was in trouble and had to defend myself. I just wanted to grab a knife and stab whoever wanted to bother me, so they'd know not to mess with me. The only way I could think to defend myself was to bring a knife. And that escalated to being arrested.

I was court-ordered to go to an immigration office, although I don't understand why. The lady there thought I couldn't speak English, but she quickly realized that wasn't the case.

"How can you speak such good English?" she asked me.

"I've been living here since I was two years old," I said.

"What are you doing here then?" she asked. For some reason she thought we were recent immigrants.

I told her I'd gotten there through the courts, due to my anger issues.

She said, "You know what? I'm going to try to help you with your case and get you to Miss Colleen."

From there, I was assigned to therapy classes, which helped me deal with my anger. I was also assigned to a six-month mandatory program called Empowered Youth. I didn't know what it was at the time.

The first time I went to the program was at Gwen Cherry Park. I felt like I just had to do my time. Do this thing for six months, then I'm out. I had to wear an ankle bracelet, which meant they could track me, so I actually had to go to the program. I was told if I graduated, they would expunge my case. So during the first few days and weeks, I was just doing my time.

But I started feeling better about the program once I got more involved. We go to different places, such as the University of Miami, and field trips on Saturdays—like one time we went shark tagging with a bunch of UM students. Another time we went to the gym to play some basketball. We've done so much that I can't even remember it all.

One of my best experiences was when Miss Colleen said I was doing so well in the program and she saw leadership in me, so she signed me up with this program called Close Up. They had four seats available on a trip to Washington, D.C., and I was fortunate to be selected.

We went to see the different monuments and memorials and we went on tours. I was in the middle school group at that time and the other three people from Empowered Youth were in the high school group. They were able to go to the White House. I wasn't able to because my plane left on Tuesday and they went on Thursday, but it was still an awesome experience.

After that I had an opportunity to meet with Commissioner Sarnoff of Coconut Grove. The same four people who had gone to D.C. were asked to help on a campaign for Commissioner Sarnoff's wife. We were paid to go door-to-door, handing out flyers and talking to people about her campaign.

I then got into a sales training program sponsored by THX Co. We sold coffee and cologne around the school and in the neighborhood. We sold the cologne for ten dollars and four of that was our profit. That job helped me with my entrepreneurial skills.

The Empowered Youth program teaches job skills, cooking skills, and entrepreneurial skills, like marketing. When I first came into the program, if someone told me to do marketing, I wouldn't have known what to do. But now I could go around to different people and tell them about the program, hand them papers, talk to them nicely, encourage them to get into the program or get involved with the program. All of this helps us to be able to get a job.

And jobs are one of the main reasons kids end up in the juvenile system—because they don't have jobs and since they grew up around drugs and violence, the first thing they think of is, I have to make money, but they don't know how and they don't have skills, so they rob. Not everybody, you know, but poverty is one of our biggest issues—that and single-parent homes.

After my six months, I went back to court and Miss Colleen spoke good about me and the things we've done and accomplished, so the court let me off probation. They removed the ankle bracelet even though I was supposed to have to wear it for a year after I finished the program. Because Miss Colleen spoke good about me, they decided to take it off then and I'm pretty sure they expunged my case.

After I finished the program in 2015, I decided to stay with Empowered Youth because I needed money to buy my own stuff and I needed a better job. I'm in the Job Development Program, currently taking chef classes and working on the truck. That's part of the program—they teach you how to get a job, so I'm taking advantage to help my future.

I've been working on the food truck, but still looking for an additional job. I found one at Surfside, a sushi place, where my mom works. I clean in the morning and the evening on Mondays and Tuesdays. I'm only in the ninth grade, so I'm still in school. But from this cleaning job, I hope to move up.

I like cooking, too. I've been doing it since I was in the fourth grade because my dad's a sushi chef. Before that, he was a chef at a steakhouse. So he learned a lot of cooking techniques, except desserts. My dad taught me a lot and now we're working on sushi and I'm learning quickly. It was hard at first, but then after four or five days, I started to get better. He taught me how to make other things, not the sushi rolls, but carpaccio and other things.

When I was younger, I was more into music and playing the guitar, but last year I started feeling like cooking was made for me, more than music. It's pretty cool. I'm hoping to get my citizenship, then get into the cooking industry, and eventually have my own restaurant. Probably a sushi and steakhouse.

My parents are a lot happier now, too, and their sacrifice to drive me across town to the program has had a good payoff. They're happy to see me following in their culinary footsteps.

Besides the job skills and opportunities, the program has taught me how to handle life situations. I know now there was a better way to handle my anger. I've learned how to stay away from trouble and how to make better decisions. What to do and what not to do. The program has taught me what's best for me and opened up my mind to the real world.

My new anger-management techniques are to either chew gum or eat candy—candy usually gets me away from it. I usually use sour patches. I realized I was thinking and worrying too much about things. For example, my mom's working all day today, so my sister stays at the house, so I worry about how she's going to be, even though I know she's going to be okay. I ate some sour patches and now I kind of forgot about it. So I use the candy or a rubber band or music. I've learned different ways to get rid of the anger or anxiety.

I'm cool with the kids in the program and at school. The kids I had problems with in middle school aren't around anymore and it makes me realize how it wasn't worth the trouble when I don't even think about them a year later. Since I've been in the program, I'm still on good terms with my old friends. I don't do the same things that they do anymore, but they still accept me.

My grades are good, but my physical science class kind of messed me up. I'm also struggling with Algebra 2. I just have to have patience for it and patience is something that I don't really have. I do after-school tutoring, but it doesn't work well with my schedule, since tutoring starts at three o'clock and I have to pick up my sister at three. So, I just try to pay attention in class as best I can or ask friends for help.

Empowered Youth really changed my life. I remember my first day. I was at Glen Cherry, sitting on the couch, and I saw all these different students come in. Then I saw Miss Colleen. She said, "Oh, you're Fernando."

Yeah. She already knew about me.

Over time, I've learned that Miss Colleen is most concerned with our environment and what's messing us up.

"How're you doing?" she'll ask. "Are you scared of something?"

She'll ask stuff like that. She's more than a coach or a mentor. She's like a mom.

CHAPTER 24

Andre,[18] EY Student

I grew up in Opa-locka and I played football for the Hurricanes and Eagles. I lived with my mother and siblings until my mom got sick and then I watched her get sicker and skinnier.

Even though I was legit, I was young and I knew a lot of stuff I wasn't supposed to know. My mom was telling me things because she felt she could talk to me since I was the oldest child in the house at the time and I was a boy. She'd be telling me I gotta be a man. She's telling me a lot of stuff, like I gotta watch out for my sisters. So I felt like I was a big boy already when I was still a kid, so I started doing things I had no business doing.

I remember going to the hospital for visits at Northshore until my momma passed away in 2004. I was about eight and my sisters don't even really remember her. One was about six and one was just a baby.

I took it hard when she died. I didn't know why she had to die and stuff. It felt like abandonment. It's not an excuse, but I got worse. My big brother wasn't always in the picture, and I didn't know my daddy. I never met him. He's from Haiti and my grandmother told me he got deported when I was little.

My grandma took over when my mom died. She adopted me and my two sisters, but not my older brother. She tried, but his daddy took him. So not only did I lose my mom, I lost my brother, too.

---

[18] All names in Andre's story have been changed to protect the family's privacy—in this chapter and throughout.

We were supposed to share holidays with my brother but every time my grandmother or auntie called his family, they got an excuse as to why my brother couldn't visit.

I was like, Forget that, and I started going over to his house instead, even though I ain't never liked his daddy. When I was there, his dad would be mad. He'd call my brother into the other room and say, "Who did you ax if he can come over here? Tell him it's time to go." It would be early, like I just got there. I felt he didn't want me around them.

Then I had my aunties and uncles. I was close to one of my aunties, but she got sent to prison. She was brought down with an indictment. That hit me hard, too, so I was wild and running around with my head off.

I was mad at everything. Well, maybe I wasn't really angry, but sad.

My trouble started in elementary school. I was a bad kid by the second or third grade. I flunked the third grade and was already doing petty stuff, like stealing bikes in the neighborhood or taking people's puppies and selling them.

We stayed in Opa-locka until I was in the sixth grade and I got kicked out of middle school. That's when my serious trouble started. My friends told me they jumped a boy and I took some of the money they took from him. I got charged with the crime even though I hadn't jumped him, but because my friends told that I had some of the money. I was charged as an accessory to a strong armed robbery and was arrested.

That was my first arrest, so I went to the place they call the JAC [Juvenile Assessment Center]. There's an area where you wait until they decide whether you get sent home or you get sent to the Department of Juvenile Justice [DJJ]. That first time they said my crime was serious, so I got shipped to DJJ for a couple of days and then released. After my arrest, I was straight and didn't get in trouble for a minute.[19]

The second time I got arrested was for petty theft when I was sixteen. I tried to steal a Levi's jacket in the mall. I put the jacket on and walked out, but two secret shoppers came up and grabbed me. "Don't run. You're caught," they said.

That was the day before a friend passed away. The day I got arrested was the day of his viewing, so I missed his viewing while I was sitting in jail. I was still a minor.

By now I was living near my brother again in the city [Liberty City] and we were both grown so no one could stop us from being together. My brother was part of the Empowered Youth program and he told me about it.

"You wanna come?" he offered one night.

I went once and I was like, This is nice! They have food and all that. So after that, when I got in trouble, I was like, "You still in that program?"

"I've about graduated already," my brother said.

"Will you mind asking that lady if she'd come to court for me?"

Miss Colleen came and tried whatever she could do, but the judge didn't really care. My crime wasn't serious enough to get sent to Empowered Youth. I was sent to another program for about four months, and did what I was sent there to do.

After that, I was stuck. My grandmother was on my back, saying, "You gotta do something! You're gonna be dead in the streets."

---

[19] A time span implying a very long time. See "for a minute," *Urban Dictionary,* www.urbandictionary.com/define.php?term=for+a+minute (accessed 12/9/16).

CHAPTER 25

Andre's grandmother knew all too well that danger lurks in the streets. The neighborhoods of northern Miami are notoriously rough. The highlights are community centers, like Gwen Cherry Park, home of the Gwen Cherry Bulls football team and Pop Warner league. People enroll their children in the programs to try to ward off trouble.

In these neighborhoods, sports is viewed as the coveted one-way ticket out of town. Sports or rap or school, but since few inner-city youth go to college, they fall back to sports. So if a person can't make it with sports, they usually feel stuck.

Boys come to the community parks to hang out or join a pick-up game. Others congregate in the back, doing or dealing drugs. The community centers are always fighting the evil forces of inner-city crime, trying to pull the youth out, but the environment keeps sucking them back in.

With drugs comes crime. One of the heaviest hit areas is Liberty City, otherwise known as "the city," which is home to the Pork 'n' Beans, one of Miami's toughest neighborhoods. Victims are shot randomly, for any reason, or no reason at all, making it a war zone right in the heart of America.

Andre

In one case, it was a woman and her mother who got shot. I don't know what the incident was, but I saw it on Facebook and the news. The daughter who got shot, she actually made a video and posted it live on Facebook. She's screaming, going all crazy, showing the gunshot wounds and she be like, "two boys with red hoodies shot me." Her momma got shot once in the arm and she got shot four times, three in the stomach and one in her arm. It was at a gas station right on 27th off of 135th.

The Lincoln Field Projects have a lot of crime activity, drugs, and robberies. Crimes used to be mostly for money, but now it's just people wanting names.[20] They're doing crimes to get recognition, like street cred.[21] It's gang mentality. They want to be top dog.

I was affiliated with a gang and I know people in a gang. You can't go to certain places, if you know it's not your boundaries. They call it "ops." That means your opposition, the people who don't like you. You can't go over there because, if you do, you might not make it back. So if you do go somewhere, you would have a gun, Tasers, a knife, Mace, or anything for protection.

Kids feel pressure to join a gang. When I grew up, that's what I saw the older people in my life doing. I thought, This must be what you gotta do. It's really tough to stand up to peer pressure and gangs. There's one of two options in a gang. You either gonna die or you're going to jail. You don't want to wait till it's too late when you go to jail or too late when you're in the grave. Peer pressure is tough, but everybody knows inside what's right and wrong.

Growing up in the city you think about whether you'll get shot, whether you'll make it out or not. If you'll get the chance to survive. For me, I just think every day about trying to stay

---

[20] The notion of respect drives gang life almost completely, and for many gang members, gaining respect means committing violent crimes. See Ed Grabianowski, "How Street Gangs Work," September 26, 2006, HowStuffWorks.com, http://people.howstuffworks.com/street-gang.htm (accessed 3/15/17).

[21] Commanding a level of respect in an urban environment due to experience in or knowledge of issues affecting those environments. See "street cred," *Urban Dictionary*, www.urbandictionary.com/define.php?term=street+cred (accessed 12/9/16).

alive. I was just living day by day and didn't see anything for my future.

I just lost a friend, Jaz, who was nineteen. We were friends since sixth grade. She got shot in Atapata. Five times, one in the head. Over the years, when you're a kid growing up in the city, you're gonna see a lot of stuff like that. You go to a lot of funerals. It's like normal to us. But when you tell other people about it, they're shocked, but to us, we're numb to it. Because it happens every day. It's just a way of life.

Not many kids play outside. A lot of people are scared to even go outside. There used to be more crime at night, but that's an old saying. Now people just don't care anymore—they shoot anytime and anywhere. It's gotten off the chain[22] a lot lately.

A lot of people like to blame crime on the music. I like to blame it on the fact that people don't want to be leaders. Everybody just wants to follow the same thing: the bad influences. Everybody who's doing the shooting and killing isn't always in a gang. It's just a follower doing it.

Kids will be outside playing and a shootout will pop off[23] in broad daylight. People will be sitting around and they can get hit for no reason. It wasn't even meant for them. Like one young girl who was just killed when a stray bullet got her in the head. She wasn't the target.

A pop off starts out of nowhere. You can just be doing something simple, like taking the trash out, and you'll get shot or you'll have to hide and take cover.

Even at the youth center and community centers, it can still pop off at any moment, if the wrong people roll up and just

---

[22] Wild, raucous, or out of control. See "off the chain," *Urban Dictionary,* www.urbandictionary.com/define.php?term=off+the+chain (accessed 12/9/16).
[23] The starting point of an event; i.e., a fight or a party. See "pop off," *Urban Dictionary,* www.urbandictionary.com/define.php?term=pop+off (accessed 12/9/16).

try to start a problem for no reason. Getting shot is as status quo as saying, "Let's go to the mall." That's why you don't walk around unless you have to.

A lot of drug activity and shootouts happen at the corner stores. A man who was just released from prison after eighteen years ran into a store with an AK-47, talking crazy. City Market is one example where the old coons hang out under the tree, drinking beer.

It's just drugs and crackheads running around. There's always either a fight breaking out, or someone's apartment getting broken into, or somebody shooting.

As long as you got the money, you can get a gun. You ain't even got to go to a store, you get one right on the street.

If you're growing up in the city and you want a gun, you get you about one hundred or two hundred dollars, go to some Old Hair,[24] and tell them you want a gun. Probably by that same day, maybe thirty minutes later, you'll have a gun in your hand. Hot off the press.

To get money for drugs or a gun, you might get it from your parents. But if you ain't got no parent who will give you money . . . like my grandma, she didn't give us much money, but what she gave I used to smoke and gamble it in school. We call it "peewee." You roll the dice, so you might come up or you might lose all your money. Sometimes your friend might be like, "Hey, bro, you wanna smoke?" You either gamble for the money or you're gonna go out there and take it by stealing or robbing.

Living here, I have a fear of surviving on a daily basis. I really wonder if I'm going to make it.

---

[24] That is, older person who's on the street or drug dealer.

CHAPTER 26

Empowered Youth tackles the key issues that oppress inner-city youth like Andre, but we face a constant challenge. No matter what magic transpires during our group sessions, life in the hood carries on undeterred. One example is the deep-seated animosity that pits police officers against African Americans. The common practice of vehicles or pedestrians being stopped for questioning without apparent cause has been coined as either driving or walking while black.

The police station was located across the street from the community center where our meetings were held at the time. On one particular evening, a new kid came to the program, which was a typical occurrence. After the class, we trickled outside to find a group of thugs awaiting the new guy. He'd crossed into enemy territory by attending the program.

The ops jumped our newbie, triggering a fighting frenzy. The boys from our program rushed to defend the new guy and the parking lot burst into pandemonium. Puny little me wrestled to the middle, trying to break up the mayhem and avert a major incident.

One of my boys called out, "Miss Colleen, you have to get away! One of those guys has a gun!" So I stepped back and pulled out my phone. My shaky fingers tapped 9-1-1.

The police station was a stone's throw from us. One vehicle pulled out in the middle of the street with his siren blaring, but no one exited the vehicle. I kept calling 9-1-1. The one car sat for about twenty more minutes, until several more backups pulled up alongside. Meanwhile, the boys continued their turf war.

* * *

Each encounter with the police in this neighborhood paints a dark picture for the boys. Their interactions can be hard to fathom. As a young black man living in the community, Andre is just one of the many teens who's been soured by repeated animosity.

Andre

I'll say the police are scared because something will pop off and they'll take a minute to come. They'll wait until they know for sure it's dead, instead of trying to intervene. By the time they come here, they have at least a body or two on the floor.

It feels like they have it programmed that if a call comes from a certain area they say, Oh no, don't respond quickly. Like they scared. But they the police; they supposed to protect.

One or two cruisers are always parked at the Pork 'n' Beans, but as much shooting as happens there, the response is always late. Their timing is ten or twenty minutes, but there's a cruiser already parked there. He should be the first one on the scene. They're scared and I don't blame them.

People don't like the police because of brutality. It's a lot of brutality we go through. I see it a lot. Me and one of my friends—I'm not gonna lie, it was pretty late—It was probably around midnight. We were walking. He came with me to see a girl and we were walking back to his house. As we're walking, a cruiser rolled up, siren came on, he cut the lights on and my friend got scared. I didn't really get scared cuz I'm like, We ain't do nothin'.

My friend like, "Oh, bro!"

I said, "Why you tripping when I know we ain't do nothin'?"

Police is like, "Come here."

I'm like, "What I did? I don't need to come over there."

"You hear what I said? You better come over here or I'm gonna make you."

My friend like, "Just do it, bro."

I'm mad cuz I know I ain't do nothin'.

He frisked us and checked us, then said, "You kids get in the house. It's too late for you to be out."

I just feel like he ain't have to do that. That was uncalled for. He just stopped and checked us for no reason. It's like if you walking with a crowd of three or more, you're likely to get stopped and frisked—it's their protocol. We could just be coming from the park. They'll ride by and they'll see us and bust that U-turn. Boom. Then you know they finna[25] come mess with us. You just gotta get ready for it. You be like, Ahhh, man. They finna come again with this bullcrap. And they just waiting for you to do any little slight thing that they don't like. They either gonna beat you up, then let you go, or they gonna take you in or try to find a reason to take you in.

Colleen

Someone who hasn't grown up in this environment might easily dismiss these encounters, and even justify them by saying that the police are trying to ensure safety on the streets. But we've also experienced some of the same treatment during our Empowered Youth program.

After our group sessions, the mentors pile kids into their vehicles to return them safely home. One evening, a mentor was driving home several passengers in his SUV when he faced the dreaded police siren. He pulled over and everyone exited the vehicle. The officer collected every license or student ID, then

---

[25] Abbreviation of "fixing to". Normally means "going to". See "finna," *Urban Dictionary*, www.urbandictionary.com/define.php?term=finna (accessed 12/9/16).

frisked and handcuffed every occupant. They were instructed to sit on the curb while the officers searched the car.

"Why are you doing this? We didn't do anything," they reasoned while the officers carried on their work in silence.

They were released an hour later, with no explanation as to why they were stopped in the first place. I've worked with police for many years and know firsthand that many want to do the right thing and they care about people. But these encounters drive a wedge between the police and the residents of inner-city neighborhoods.

The police can't make arrests in some neighborhoods because citizens won't come forward. Perhaps foot patrol could improve their relationship with law-abiding citizens while deterring the criminals with visible police presence. In any case, resolving criminal behavior is a significant challenge. The ultimate deterrent is retribution, yet a stunning 95 percent of the crimes are left unsolved.

This contentious relationship with the police is one more element working against my kids. But if we can break down those hostilities so people really understand one another as people, we could achieve real community. We've had police officers join our circle groups and they'll say, "I have a three-year-old at home. I want to go home to my family." Those positive interactions help the boys understand that the officer also has something to lose in every encounter. *Everybody* wants to make it home to their family.

Our goal is to break down the barriers of race and position, because if everyone stays in their own camps and continues to judge the other person, then we can never make progress. Humanizing both sides is the only real answer.

I tell the kids that so much of what happens to them is really up to them. It's about their choices and decisions. Yes, people might be reacting to them in a certain unpleasant way, but the outcome ultimately starts with their own actions.

We as mentors have got to be aware and even assimilate into their culture. With rival gang members in the group, we minimize skirmishes by creating a neutral space during our meetings. I've become fluent in street language and enjoy interjecting it into their cryptic conversations. "Listen, dude, that's a really bad idea. Don't be doing that," I'll say and then they'll know I deciphered their code.

It's the same for the rap music that assaults the airwaves whenever we transport the boys. I'll say, "I don't like Drake's new song, do you?" That kind of question will usually be followed by a long heavy silence.

* * *

CHAPTER 27

Andre

After I finished my court-ordered program, I was stuck. I needed to do something. I used to go to Miami Central School, but I really wasn't doing what I was supposed to, so I ended up at Stellar Leadership Academy on 79th.

Stellar's a computer-based alternative school and you graduate at your own pace. They take kids from age fifteen to twenty-one. But they still give a high school diploma, so that's why I wanted to go there. It's like a second chance, and if you still can't get it together, then you just gotta get a GED.

I visited the Empowered Youth program with my brother before, and I liked it, so when I got done with my court-ordered program, I called up Miss Colleen and was like, "Is it okay if I come to your program?" She welcomed me with open arms.

When Miss Colleen gave me a job on the food truck, it was my first real job with a paycheck. At first it was hard learning the menu. I was like, "What go with that again?" or "What this come with?" But then it got easier. The menu comes from things we already made in chef class. The chef lets us pick who cooks and who works the window, so we talk about that before we open. But we all do every job on the truck.

One time, Miss Colleen told me to smile more when I was working the window. I just said, "Thank you, Miss." I thought maybe I'm not smiling enough or maybe I need to smile more so I don't look scary or like I'm from the hood cuz I already got dreads and tattoos.

One tattoo is a mural for my mom, and another is her name. I have three crosses for Calgary, where Jesus died, one that says "Forgiveness," and I got "Blessed" cuz I feel like I'm blessed. I got "Long live Jaz" for my homegirl that died. I got "Loyalty" cuz loyalty means so much to me and it's a strong word. I also got clouds, a dove, and a gun.

But since Miss Colleen gave me a job, I've met a lot of people and I talk to them easy. It wasn't something I would have done before. Since I started working on the truck, I felt like I could go ask someone else for a job if I needed one. I'm like, "Excuse me. How you doing? Is the manager here? Is y'all guys hiring?" They say, "Put in an application." So, I do that a lot now. Before I wasn't doing that. I've applied at places like Auntie Anne's in Overtown. Macy's warehouse, and Lowe's.

Through the program, I made a résumé and wrote articles for the newspaper. I don't know if they ever made it [got published], but mine was about a local artist named Little J because I like his music.

The things we do in the program taught us a lot of pointers about life. We have sessions with college students, and they really don't got it all together yet either, so sometimes we could tell them stuff that helped them out.

I joke about coming to the program for the pizza, but I really come for the conversation. We be talking about some good stuff on Monday and Wednesday nights.

Some of the boys can be a tough cookie to cut. I see it all the time at the program. They say, "Put your phone up," or "Take your hat off." I know it already. Some boys have a hard time doing the basic stuff, the easy stuff. It's not that hard. The requirements are really common knowledge, like when you walk into a building, take your hat off. Pull your pants up—no sagging. Don't be on your phone, and have it on vibrate. A lot of the boys don't want to do it. They're a work in progress.

As for myself, I'm planning to get my diploma, then try to find a job. I wasn't really thinking about college. I don't think

I'm the right person for it. I'm liking the cooking thing now. We have a new chef and he went to [Le] Cordon Bleu, so I'm like, I might be able to do that. He said it only took eighteen months, so I can think about that.

Since I've been in the program, I finally started seeing hope for my future.

CHAPTER 28

I'm constantly observing and giving corrective feedback to the boys, especially when they're working on the truck. One way I judge my success is by the feedback of our customers. It always pleases me when people refer to the boys as gentlemen, because that's an important goal of mine.

I tell the boys they can be whomever they want to be when they're in the hood, but when they're out in the general public, they're expected to be respectful. We work on basic common courtesies, such as saying "please" and "thank you."

An inner-city kid with a tough facade creates a negative perception. But sometimes a few minor tweaks to smooth out their razor-sharp edges are all it takes to leave a lasting positive impression instead.

A simple thing like smiling while working the window of the food truck boosts customer satisfaction. Andre was one of those kids with a stiff poker face who needed to exude a little more sunshine. After my impromptu feedback, he flashed his dazzling set of pearly whites. In one instant, his hardened features softened, making him more approachable.

Andre accepted my corrective feedback perfectly, but some of the kids cop a serious attitude. Human nature is resistant to change, but it also goes back to the boys' formation.

The majority of their parents were never married. There's a "baby momma" or "baby daddy" culture that doesn't encourage commitment or formalized marriage. Often they live with either their moms or grandmas. Their father says he'll visit them, but he's said that every Saturday for years, and he never makes it.

Children learn through doing and these kids end up with a fractured sense of what's right and wrong. They develop no sense of accountability or responsibility. People surrounding and influencing them are always doing what's best for themselves and that's what my kids learn. They don't learn how their actions can hurt others, because they're often raised and shaped by inconsiderate, insensitive, unloving people.

For a child who's never seen a commitment kept, he never learns the value of keeping one. Later, when it comes to loyalty for things like showing up for work on time, he has no examples or framework to draw upon. It's a foreign concept that needs extensive reinforcement and guidance to establish any foundation.

One of my students, who shall remain nameless, is a perfect example of a work in progress. During one session, our youth facilitator brought a video he uses in the school system for sex education.

Soon after the video began, nervous, uncomfortable laughter filled the room. It was the classic reaction to camouflage the boys' discomfort. When the video came to a section about AIDS, it showed two men walking hand-in-hand and then cuddling.

My little fourteen-year-old student launched into full-fledged melodrama. What he lacks in stature, he makes up for with attitude. He covered his face with his hands. "NO, NO, NO!" he cried. "This is terrible, I can't watch this!" Then he ran from the room.

I found his reaction to be the ultimate hypocrisy. My kids have broken the law, which conjures all kinds of preconceived notions and judgments about them. For this student to display such narrow-mindedness and intolerance was inexcusable.

"Listen," I told him later. "You don't have to date them, but you can't judge them. It's not your business or your choice. As long as they don't approach you, just leave it alone."

And thus began a futile debate with a petulant teen. We volleyed back and forth. "Miss Colleen, that's unnatural," he said, while contorting his face.

My little rebel had recently begun working on the food truck, which meant he was representing the program to the public. At the time, the truck was stationary at Wynwood Yard in the Art District in Miami, home of a notoriously diverse population. So I pulled the student off the work schedule. He was visibly upset when he asked me why.

"You're not on the schedule because you could easily have two guys walk up to the van and ask you for a hamburger," I responded. "They could be standing in front of the window cuddling up and holding hands and kissing. I can't take a chance at what you might say to them. That's not who we are. You're an at-risk young man who has a lot of judgment leveled against you, and you can't do the same thing to other people. And you're not going to represent our program by saying some remark or making a face to insult them. I'm not taking that chance."

He was furious, of course. "I'm not coming to the program anymore," he threatened.

"I'm sorry you feel that way," I responded, "but you're only hurting yourself as long as you continue to be intolerant. You can't treat people the way people treat you."

I play this constant tug-of-war against a mindset that's perpetuated through generations. The prejudices and beliefs are often deep-rooted.

I tried to explain to the student that, in real life, this same guy could save his life one day. He could be his boss or his neighbor or his banker. "You can't just cut off the world based on what your narrow view of the world looks like," I tried to reason.

It's an ongoing challenge to pry their minds open and insert a new idea. But if they can't rid themselves of these destructive notions, they won't be able to assimilate into mainstream life.

In their distorted social paradigm, a single mom tries to control her son, who's seeking maleness out on the street, in all the wrong places. Oftentimes she can't rein him in. Parents literally go into the public attorney's office and ask, "Will you take my kid? I can't control him." They've given up to a great extent. Moms are simply worn down.

By the time the boys get to me, the family's pretty disengaged, which also leads to another challenge. If the boy makes a positive change in his life, he needs acknowledgment and support from home.

Many grandmothers step in for absent parents. They're doing their best, but they're overwhelmed, tired, and burnt out. One particular grandmother was awarded her grandchildren because her son is in federal prison and the mother of the children was a mess. Now in her late 70s or early 80s, the grandmother's raising a host of kids, after raising her own. She's trying to manage several youngsters, but she sees one grandson drifting off the way her son in prison did. Two other grandsons were killed in gang violence. Another one has been in prison. The child in my program is the next one in line, then there are four younger kids in the six- to ten-year-old range. The grandmother's worn out and at wit's end.

What kind of stability can youth in this environment possibly have?

From the child's perspective, it's very confusing. He must feel rejected and abandoned. From the grandmother's perspective, all her kids are dying and going to prison, and now here's another one going down the tubes. When you mix these dynamics together, there's a tremendous amount of confusion, disappointment, heartbreak, and rejection. Like a toxic stew made from rotten ingredients. That's often the only environment my kids know.

We often take the boys to the McDonald's in Liberty City, where I get a glimpse into typical family dynamics. One young mother left a lasting impression. She was probably in her late teens, already with two children. The older child was about five or six years old and a toddler was latched onto the mother's legs. Clearly frustrated, she was shaking him off. "Get the fuck away from me," she told him.

Unfortunately my own boys hail from similar family dynamics and lack of support. One example is Darnell.[26] He was referred to the program by his school counselor. Darnell was a sweet lost soul and all he wanted was a family. He wasn't a criminal and didn't mean anyone harm. He was floundering in school and getting into petty trouble when I met him, but he was genuinely a good guy. His goal was to attend college.

Darnell really took to the mentors and bonded with one of my board members, who ended up taking Darnell into his home. The experience was wonderful for Darnell, who yearned for the father he never had. The board member and his wife welcomed Darnell into their empty nest, where they loved and treated him as their own son.

Darnell loved to cook and developed serious talent between his training at Empowered Youth and cooking with his surrogate family at home. Outside the hood, he was exposed to a whole new world, including a different variety of music. Pavarotti's operas struck a chord with Darnell and he set one as his cellphone ringtone.

Nothing came easy for him, but with hard work, Darnell overcame several obstacles and was accepted into the army. He

---

[26] Name has been changed to protect the privacy of the family.

decided to treat his birth family to a farewell dinner before leaving for basic training.

His beautiful spread included filet of sole and fresh asparagus, but his family was less than impressed. No one would touch it since it wasn't fried. "What are these green things? This is horrible!" They scoffed at his food, then later, when Pavarotti announced an incoming phone call, Darnell took more ribbing. "What is *that*? You're a *white* boy now?"

Darnell's thoughtful parting gift fizzled. When his surrogate father arrived the next morning to pick him up, Darnell dropped into the car, destroyed. "I can't go back, I don't belong there anymore," he said.

Darnell's story is bittersweet. He wanted more out of life but didn't have a clue how to get it. Through the program and with mentoring, he was able to distance himself from the negative influences and went on to pursue a career of his dreams.

When my boys start to grow and separate themselves from the hood mentality, they're often punished for it. Thankfully, the human spirit is amazingly resilient, so kids like Darnell aren't a lost cause.

The resilience reveals itself in many ways. A relaxing afternoon outing is one simple example. While our group was lounging at the beach one day, I ended up seated on the sand with Anthony, one of the youngest boys. With the sharp wind whipping across us, I wrapped the little guy into the sweater I was wearing and we sat nestled together, watching people stroll the beach.

"Good morning," I started saying to each passerby while Anthony kept looking up at me, studying me. I finally answered his unasked question. "I think it's nice to be friendly and say 'good morning' to people."

"Good morning!" my little parrot shouted out to the next passerby, melting my heart.

Our youth are impressionable. They develop a vocabulary based on what they hear, whether it's "Get the fuck off me," or "Good morning." I'm making sure that what my kids hear is "Good morning."

CHAPTER 29

I can't do what I do alone and I'm fortunate to have a steady stream of help in many forms. One of our critical key roles in the program is the youth facilitator, whose role is to plan and manage our meetings.

Our current youth facilitator, Calvin, was a valuable addition to the team.

Calvin, Youth Facilitator

As a child, I was fortunate to be involved with a program called Youth Expressions, where my interest in art, rap, creative writing, and poetry were all encouraged. But beyond those passions, I wasn't sure what I wanted to do with my life. After high school, I accepted a position at Youth Expressions, pleased to serve an organization that had helped me grow as a young person and an artist.

My path at Youth Expressions sparked an interest in youth development, where group facilitation and similar roles provided an avenue for reaching young people.

One day a gentleman from my poetry community told me about an opportunity at Empowered Youth as a group facilitator. I was familiar with Empowered Youth, but only as a bystander. I didn't know the specifics of the program, but had come to know Colleen's face well.

I'd seen the group out in the community in various forums and youth-related conferences. I worked at the Belafonte TACOLCY Center, where Empowered Youth used to hold evening meetings, so I would see the group gathering whenever I left work late.

At the time I learned about the youth facilitator role, I was working at the high school and also planning my wedding. I wasn't sure I'd have time for another commitment, but I attended a meeting to check things out and decide if I could handle the extra load.

During that first meeting, I observed the one-sided group dynamics. The disengaged teens slouched back in their seats. Once the meeting was in progress, I tried my hand at engaging them in conversation and they eagerly opened up.

The demographic was very familiar to me. That first night, two students from my high school sat among the group of boys. Seeing them felt like a sign that we're all interconnected and I was completing a circle. My own school's students might get in trouble and end up in jail or in a program like Empowered Youth. Maybe if I was working on both ends of this spectrum, I would gain greater insight into the needs of these young men.

Colleen offered me the position and I felt I could help, so I accepted. I expected it to be a challenge and was painfully correct. I went home and told my wife, "I'm not sure how long I'm going to be there. This is *tough*. I figured it would be, but this is *really* tough."

Meanwhile, a year and a half has flown by since that first meeting. I've developed real connections with the boys and enjoyed several pivotal experiences.

I'm from the same community and I still work in the same community, two circumstances that help me relate to the boys. Their situations aren't foreign to me. But even when you're from where they're from, even when you look like they look, even when you've had a lot of the same experiences, you're still *not* them. You don't know them as individuals. You don't know their specific life experiences and how that's brought them to where they are. You have to take all those things into account.

I knew I wouldn't be able to handle each of these young men exactly the same way. We wouldn't all form the same relationships, because there's no cookie-cutter approach to youth development, especially in this sort of demographic.

After spending time with the group, I built relationships and gained the boys' trust. Once I'd established myself, I implemented simple ground rules to create structure and consistency. Once habits are established, they're not rules anymore. They're just protocol.

One of my roles as youth facilitator is to run our group meetings. One day I decided to open our session by encouraging everyone to share something positive about their week. We coined it "Positive Shares" and incorporated the practice into our routine.

Each attendee shares anything that happened since the last time we met, whether it be big or small. Something as inconsequential as, "I started a new series on Netflix," or "I found a sock that I've been missing for a week." The purpose is to teach the boys to find things to celebrate, no matter how terrible life may feel. One young man shares the same thing each time, saying, "I woke up this morning." That's a perfect celebration.

The first day I forgot to open the meeting with Positive Shares, two hands popped into the air. "Calvin, we didn't do the Positive Shares, and I have something to say," one boy said. "Yeah, that's exactly what I was going to say," the other boy added. Several others from the group agreed.

Wow, this is awesome, I thought. They showed me I was establishing a bond and consistency with the group. These kids didn't want to talk when I first met them. Now they're engaged, sharing, laughing, and bonding with each other. I knew we had to continue the Positive Shares.

I felt I was making inroads by adding structure to the program and establishing myself within the group. My authority was tested one evening when a verbal altercation between two kids quickly escalated. Tension flooded the room.

My experience with this type of intervention had taught me that if I stood and got between the boys, I would validate the threat, intensify the confrontation, and trigger a fight.

Instead, I remained seated and cracked a joke, then asked the boys to sit down. And they did! I was able to make one of them laugh, while the other stewed quietly. The thick tension evaporated.

What I appreciated most was that none of the bystanders aggravated the situation, as I was certain they would've done when I first joined the group. Originally, I would have foreseen the boys taking sides and instigating an all-out brawl. No one did that. In fact, they berated the troublemakers, calling out, "Sit down, man, we're about to get started!"

Once I'd established myself, I began getting input from mentors. These people give freely of themselves, lending a voice and a listening ear, to help wherever they can. So when they make suggestions, we implement any that might be helpful.

One female mentor from the community had done well for herself and wanted to give back on behalf of her brothers, who'd been in trouble. Her strong personality didn't overshadow her compassion for the young men.

She suggested a cell phone policy to be used during meetings. I figured it wouldn't work, but I couldn't deny we clearly struggled to keep the boys off their phones. Our mentor offered to bring a box that would be used to store all the phones during each session. We'd give it a try.

Of course the boys were initially upset, but eventually everyone jumped on board and began putting their phones in the box when they entered the room.

When the mentor stopped attending the meetings, the boys asked me, "Are we still doing the box?" Even though they didn't like it, they were accustomed to the familiar routine. So I started bringing a box.

The beautiful thing is that once you create a culture, everyone who walks into the place will assimilate to the environment. They follow the behavior of the individuals who are already there.

For example, a new kid was considering becoming part of Empowered Youth and came to a meeting for the first time. When we were ready to start, I asked everyone for their phone. The new boy looked up, stunned. His eyes scanned the room. In that pivotal moment, if he saw other kids unwilling to give up their phones, he wouldn't give up his. But when he saw his peers willingly walk over and place their phone in the box, newbie did, too.

Each small yet powerful example is a reminder that the culture is set. We see the same thing repeatedly. A new kid enters the room. He's quiet and reserved. He's got the hardened look that says, I've been through this before. I know exactly what this program is. I refuse to be friendly. I'm not going to be open. I don't want anybody to think I'm soft.

Then, within fifteen minutes, they see everybody laughing and joking. The same kids who have a criminal charge of some sort are bonding with each other. Even the toughest and most aggressive-looking ones are joking and playing around. The open and light environment encourages the boys to open up quickly.

Chapter 30

Calvin, Youth Facilitator

Of all the defining moments I've experienced while working with Empowered Youth, the most powerful came from watching one particular young man grow as an individual. Darryl[27] struggled to make difficult changes in his life, but as he matured, he gave advice and guidance to the other boys, like a big brother.

Darryl lived with his ailing grandparents while he was on probation. Probation restrictions are difficult for anyone, but especially for an impulsive teen who wants to hang with his friends or run to the store whenever he wants.

One day Darryl's grandfather passed out in a park, near their home, but Darryl needed permission before leaving the house to help. Desperate to check on his grandfather, Darryl called his parole officer, then anyone else he could think of, to get permission to go. When he couldn't reach anyone, he left the house on instinct.

Darryl faced a six-year prison sentence for his parole violation and a trial date was set. As one of the Empowered Youth contingent who attended his pretrial, I was astounded to hear the prosecutors describe him as a menace to society and accuse him of tricking everybody. "He needs to be incarcerated or he'll hurt someone," they told the judge.

For those of us who knew Darryl, it was like, Really? Are we talking about the same person? I know this kid and we cannot possibly be talking about the same kid.

---

[27] Name has been changed to protect the privacy of the family.

We rallied support and attended his court date. It was helpful for the judge and prosecutor to see several people sitting in court on behalf of this young man, including two lawyers and the CEO and program facilitator of Empowered Youth, three of whom were middle-aged white people. The presence of those three made a major impact because they're of the demographic who might normally be scared of this kid or who might assume he's a thug, gangster, or predator. But instead, they were there on his behalf.

Usually, the mom and other family members would show their support and say what a wonderful person the accused is. But anyone's mom *has* to say their kid is good, that he's just having a tough time. By contrast, the presence of our Empowered Youth team clearly showed Darryl had a true support system.

The judge listened to all ten of us who came to support Darryl, and I knew he didn't have to do that. In the end, he gave Darryl another shot.

After the hearing, my wife and I agreed to take Darryl home, because he didn't have a ride. As we left the courthouse, he got a call that his family was being evicted. They were packing up their belongings when we dropped Darryl off.

We grabbed dinner from McDonald's, but within the thirty minutes it took us to return with food for Darryl, he was gone.

The neighbor informed us that Darryl's parole officer called him, saying he was supposed to meet her at the office after the court hearing. If he wasn't there by a certain time, she would consider it a violation of his parole. I was upset because I knew they hadn't told him that at the courthouse.

He hadn't been out of jail for an hour and was already in danger of going back.

To make matters worse, a U-Haul truck was waiting by the time Darryl returned home. The eviction that he thought was forthcoming was actually that evening. Without a place to stay, he would be in violation of his probation.

So my wife and I debated what to do. No, we argued.

She pleaded, "We can't let him go back to jail. You said you love these kids, and if you really love them, we've got to do this."

"We have a six-year-old, we have no idea what to do with a teenager! Are you thinking this through?" I asked her.

"Of course I'm thinking this through! It's the right thing to do," she insisted.

After a heated volley, we sat quietly with our own thoughts. I already knew that any other family members Darryl had wouldn't provide the healthiest environment for him. I wasn't sure how it could work out, but I couldn't see him go back to jail, so I gave in.

Darryl lived with us for the next four or five months. He's a great kid and it was an amazing experience. I connected with him on another level. It was one of the most powerful experiences I've had as part of Empowered Youth and it's something I never thought I would have done, and probably wouldn't have if it wasn't for my wife's big heart.

At the time, Darryl was working on his GED and he has since completed it. He now has a baby on the way and is currently looking for a job.

It's a struggle for these kids on a daily basis, as Darryl's story shows. It's the same thing I see with the kids at school. I can talk to them about critical thinking and deductive reasoning but when they go home, it's a whole different set of expectations. Like when you go to therapy, they say you have to remember that *you* went to therapy, not the people around you. You can take all the things you learned in therapy home with you, but it doesn't mean it will work, because those people weren't in therapy. You're trying to implement new ideas to people who haven't had the training or guidance that you have had. This is the boys' struggle. They may try to make some changes or do something different, but then they go back out into the community where everything is the same as it was.

It's a hard tide to swim against. I can tell them that I'm from where they're from all I want, but the fact that I'm not in their shoes at the moment, it makes me less relatable. That's a constant challenge. It's an ongoing struggle to get them to see things and implement things when they're not around me.

A lot of these kids don't have an opportunity to just be kids, which is another thing I like about the program. The field trips to the beach, for basketball or football, or other events, gives them the opportunity to enjoy being a kid without having the responsibility of taking care of a little brother or sister or mom.

We have so many successes in the program, but you also have to accept the reality that you're not capable of saving everybody. Maybe someone else will reach them—maybe a teacher, coach, or family member. I'm not Superman. I may plant a seed that someone else will water and nurture.

The program isn't an exact science and it might not work for everybody, but it's about giving kids in need an opportunity. Locking them up and throwing away the key just doesn't fix it.

CHAPTER 31

Calvin has splendidly fine-tuned the structure of the program and our adult volunteers assist him to ensure every group session makes a positive lasting impression on the boys.

At the beginning of each meeting I like to introduce the new mentors or visitors, and sometimes they take a few minutes to address the group.

When mentors Terrance and Darius[28] were introduced, they imparted their hard-earned life lessons on our youth.

Terrance, Mentor

I'm going to give y'all a quick rundown on how I met Darius. I met him in prison. We became real good friends cuz in prison, it's called havin' each other's back. He's from Overtown and I'm from Scott Projects and we just clicked. Just because we was in prison, that didn't mean we had to keep doing the things that we came to prison for. So we changed our minds and said, "Look, man, we finna do something else. Cuz we ain't coming back here."

Me and him been together almost a decade now. No charges, no trouble, and that's why we're here today.

[Applause from the crowd drowned out anything more Terrance had to say, and Darius grabbed the lead.]

---

[28] Both names are changed to respect the privacy of their families.

Darius, Mentor

We growed up with violence. So we made a pact and a bond with a few other dudes from Miami that nobody was gonna try us up.

I did a lot of time at a young age, when I was probably a little older than y'all. I was going through the everyday motions and a lot of times you gonna feel homesick. From what I know, you guys are on probation and ya'll in a program to try to help you to possibly do something different in your life. I can't even say "change" cuz when I got out of prison I didn't have change on my mind. Whatever the means to make money was, that's what I was gonna do. Right?

I did six years and when I first got out, I was thinking, What can I do? What do I know how to do? The only thing I did know how to do was what they taught me in there. They taught me how to cut grass and tree trimming, but who gonna hire a felon? Go try to fill in applications and they knock you down.

But then somebody may give you a shot and say, "Okay, you can work for me. You can show me what you can do." They don't know what your record is or what the charges is, but if they ain't gonna hire you, then what you gonna do? You gonna sell dope? Gonna rob? You're gonna do whatever it is to make means. To make money, right?

If you're here, then you're still living. I know it's an everyday struggle. But if you're still here, it means you still got a shot. You still got a chance.

Even with Terrance, we ain't from the same neck of the woods. Matter of fact, before I met him, Overtown never dealt with the city [Liberty City], like the city ain't deal with us. But when you're in a certain spot when all you got is yourself, you ain't gonna have no choice but to put down whatever animosity you have for each other. And we didn't even know why we didn't like each other, it's just that he was from the city and I'm from

Overtown. The older guys we looked up to while we were growing up, that's what they told us.

We don't fuck with niggers out the city. Or, we don't fuck with niggers from Overtown. That's what they told us and that's what we went by. Same coaches y'all deal with right now. We don't fuck with the other side.

We were cold killers, if he crossed my path on the street and I ain't known him. He would have done the same thing to me. I'm glad that a higher power, which is Father God to me, changed my mind state and made me see different from the stuff that I'd been through. I don't know if you guys believe in a higher power, but I hope you do.

I'm glad I found a higher power cuz a lot of times I ain't see no future in something gonna change. Something gonna change for the better for me and something gonna change for the better for my homeboy.

Like, after we got out, there was times when we probably got like twenty dollars between us. I'd say, "I'm gonna come over to your house and give you ten." And I got ten, just so my homeboy won't think to go rob somebody again, where he'll have to go back in there. Cuz it would hurt me. I know this person now. I know him on a one-on-one basis.

I know he's a good person overall, but if you're standing in front of a courtroom in front of a bunch of strangers, they don't know you, brother. They don't know you. They don't know how good you is. They don't know if you take care of your household. They don't know if you're a good brother to your little brother or sister. They don't know if you're a good son to your momma or your daddy. A good grandson. They don't know that. All they know is, three counts of armed robbery with a firearm. They're looking at a piece of paper.

When they're looking at you, you're a threat to our society and you ain't going to go against the rules and the laws.

Even here, I see they got the phone box where you put your phones. That's showing you guys structure, man. It's gotta be structure for anything. Even when you're incarcerated, it's structure there. If you violate that, you go to the box.

Me and him, we went to the box a whole couple of times. He had a coat and tried to sneak me stuff in the box. I'm about to go crazy and he's trying to tell me, "Calm down, buddy, you're gonna be all right."

I said, "No, I ain't gonna be all right! I'm in jail in jail! How you gonna be in jail in jail?"

I ain't gonna lie to you, man, it was hard. I tell you no lie right now. I went into prison for nine felonies. Three counts of slash-and-grab burglary, three counts of grand theft over a hundred thousand, and grand theft auto and resisting arrest.

Now I got free time and I'm tired. I got a headache cuz I'm so tired, but I work three jobs. I told my supervisor that a friend said I should check out a volunteering thing, about some young guys that got in trouble, like myself. I wanted to come and see how it worked, cuz I don't remember having this as a youngster, not in Miami.

Terrance

They have the JAC [Juvenile Assessment Center] now. There was none of that back then. It went: you get caught, you're going to the county jail. Then, if he's old enough to do the crime, send him to prison. That was it. They didn't have this type of stuff right here.

A prison number is a prison number. It doesn't matter. When you get out, it's gonna be a prison number. That's actually your new name. I wanna get that understood. 19992531,[29] that's

---

[29] Number has been changed to protect the privacy of the family.

his new name. You can still go by the name that you're momma gave you, but your prison number is actually your new name, plus your social security number. When you type your name and social security number on a job application, your crime's gonna come up. Period. Like, he's a felon and this is what he did.

I was observing you guys as you came in the room tonight and I apologize, but I ain't shake none of your hands. I just wanted to look at y'all. Not to pass any judgement, I just wanted to look at the mirror reflection on how I was at y'all's age. I'm like, He looks like he's about twelve, and that's when it started for me. It started in elementary, being defiant to all the teachers. I think the first time I got suspended from elementary was in the first grade. My momma was upset saying, "How can ya'll be telling me you want to suspend a six-year-old?" But she didn't know that when she wasn't there, and I'm in the presence of these friends, I'm doing it the worst and the most of all. Whatever it is, I'm doing it.

I do suffer from addictions. I still suffer from addiction to the street life, because I did it for so long. When I still pass by in the city in Overtown and I still see homeboys that still ain't making it, sometimes it does something to me, especially when you jump out and they like, "Terrance! What's up, boy? Hey!" And you jump out and hollering at your homeboys and you reminisce on the past, you think, man, I miss this here, but I work now. I'm doing something different now.

You gotta stay with that mindstate, cuz if you don't, you're gonna be lost out here. If Father God can help you get at least to twenty-five or thirty years old, it will be a game changer. That's where the real game changer was at for me. I remember a math teacher of mine told me I wouldn't make it to twenty-one, going the way I was going. I was seventeen at the time. But I still made it. Being shot. Shooting back. I ain't got caught for that, but you still get caught for something. Selling dope? I ain't got caught for that but I still got caught for something. The snatch-and-grab burglary, that was something I did for fun. That was the crime they were *not* gonna catch me for. They might catch me for the dope, cuz I'm riding around with three, four, or five ounces. Well, they might catch me with this money, or they might catch me with this gun, but I ain't worried about no burglary. We do that for fun. And that's what got me sunk. That's what got me caught.

Now I feel that whatever happened in my life, Father God designed it that way. I had two guys who got away clean. Now the question is, was I gonna tell on these people who was with me? Hell, we went as a crew. But every man was for theyself in this burglary that we committed. You gonna tell on these people or you gonna keep it g?[30] That goes with the rule of being in the street. We don't tell nobody.

So guess what? Even if I was scared where these people gonna send me, I couldn't say a word. And I wasn't gonna say a word, cuz I really committed myself to the street stuff.

I see you got an ankle monitor on, so I know you're walking a thin line. I remember wearing one of those and cutting that damn thing off. See, like nothing you could do is new now, it's all the same. I remember having the dreads and the golds like y'all do. I met this doctor and she asked me, "You wanna take out the golds and get yourself a new look?"

"Well, naw, cuz it would take away my street look," I said.

But sometimes you need the help from people. Don't think y'all don't need this help. Y'all sometimes need a little

---

[30] To maintain a level of respect for oneself and those around you, similar to how those of a "gangsta" background earn respect through their actions and by not disrespecting others of a similar background. See "keep it g," *Urban Dictionary,* www.urbandictionary.com/define.php?term=keep%20it%20g (accessed 3/15/17).

guidance to a better life, a better prize. I know y'all probably dealing with everyday struggles, like, my daddy's not around, momma don't seem concerned, cuz she's got a couple other kids, but it will be better for you if you just be patient and hold on.

When we got out, I started selling drugs, cuz that's all I knew. I was illiterate when I went to prison. I couldn't read, write, or spell. It's a lady named Miss Sonda, she was my private attorney. She felt so bad for me. I was fourteen years old. The judge asked me to sign a paper and Miss Sonda asked me, do I understand what I was signing?

"I can't read that," I told her.

Why couldn't I read? Cuz I didn't listen when I was your age. I didn't want to listen to the teachers. I thought it was so cool to skip school. This is what the streets is feeding us. Instead of the older guys telling you to go to school, to go do something, they say, "Man, go sell this pack for me. You want a couple J's?[31] You want that new outfit?" We get so caught up in this material stuff and this is what society is feeding y'all right now. Y'all want everything that you see the dope boy do.

This is not a game, gentleman. Like Miss Colleen said, we can't want it more than you want it. We ain't gotta be the one on probation, we ain't got no monitors on our ankles. Nobody's watching us. Ya'll gotta take this advice and run with it.

So it's ya'll choices and decisions. It's about the right choice to make. We left the streets in 1998, and when we go down 15th Avenue and 18th Avenue, those dudes are still doing the same thing. Half of them asking *us* for money. I'm like, You a dope boy and you asking *me* for money? What're you sellin'? Dreams?

It's a trap, man. I'm telling you it's not a game. You gotta listen. This might seem boring right now. It might seem like this

---

[31] That is, a joint of marijuana.

nigger's trippin'. These people here are giving you a chance right now to turn it around. And it's not gonna happen overnight.

I did all that time and still got out and went to selling drugs. But I'm telling you, it gets old. You get tired of running from the police. You get tired wondering if he's gonna shoot you in the head. You get tired of looking over your shoulder. Do something different, man.

Take this here. Act like SpongeBob and soak this stuff up, man. You don't have to have everything the streets have. It seems cool right now, but it's nothing but material stuff. That's what I had to get between my head. That's all I was robbing and stealing for was material things.

If you ain't got the latest, what everybody else got, oh well. You'll get it later. Just work hard. Go do something.

CHAPTER 32

Darius[32] and Terrance are mentors who fully understand the world from the perspective of our young men, because their journey began in the same shoes. Except these men's lives derailed and then they paid the judicial price. Now they're encouraging our young men to take a straighter track than they did. Even with their admitted continual pull of the streets, men like Darius and Terrance rise above.

Their powerful presentation to the youth proves the advantage of having mentors from all walks of life. Everyone contributes something different and valuable.

During each session, an interactive activity is planned, then moderated by Calvin. The larger group breaks out into small clusters and the mentors disperse among the boys for the planned discussion of the evening. An assigned meeting facilitator takes command after the introductions are made. As one example, Laura, a young and vibrant attorney, takes over the lead.

Laura, Mentor

You all tell incredible stories. You may not even know you're doing it. Today is not so much about writing, but telling your story and talking about your challenges.

One of the things that upsets us lawyers is that kids in the criminal justice system can be treated like adults. Kids as young as fourteen years old, they can be sentenced to life in prison. There are some bills in the legislature that can actually change

---

[32] All names in this chapter have been changed to respect the privacy of the group participants.

how we treat young people. If we're going to try to change hearts and minds, there's nothing more powerful than words.

Having heard from Terrance and Darius you *feel* something, you see they've been through something and they learned a lesson from it. And the thing is, y'all have stories like that. Stories change lives and they start movements.

In the civil rights movement, what story told so many people that they need to think differently? Rosa Park's story. Stories are incredibly powerful at changing the world.

So what I want to do today is start developing our stories of self. Stories about a challenge, a choice, an outcome, and a lesson. Four pieces about something you've been through.

Today is really just about talking through all the pieces. If you go through your challenge, we can bounce off each other, ask questions, and give feedback. Explain it in a detailed way so we can develop the pieces. I know that when Terrance speaks, he's got the details down. And the details are what really bring it home to me.

The last time he spoke, he said, "I know there are 397 bricks on a prison wall. That's because I spent seven years counting them." It's been over a week since I heard that sentence but it hit me in a way like . . . you know how really good music hits you? That's what a really good story can do. That's what really good words can do.

Today you're going to start with your story. Pick one specific situation—one important piece—and really get into the detail. Maybe you can think about the exact situation that led you to be in this program or something else that had a meaningful impact on your life. Something that made a major shift or left a lasting memory.

So once you identify your challenge, then describe the choice you made. What did you decide to do in that situation?

Then describe the outcome of your decision. How did it play out? What was the result? And then the lesson is what you learned.

In your small groups, you'll discuss it in detail. By detail, I mean things like who was there? What did you do? What was the color of the building you went into? What are some specific things you can remember about it? The more articulate you can be and the more imagery you have in your story, the clearer the picture you will paint through your words, and the more it affects another person, because you bring them into that situation.

Like we just said, 397 bricks. The first thing I think of is these 397 bricks. In my head, I'm seeing it. That's imagery.

So after you write the short details, we'll go back and start to really build on the story.

We're going to take about ten minutes for silent writing for everybody to write to themselves. Write out a challenge, the choice that you made, the outcome, and the lesson.

[The boys are engaged but need more guidance, and the mentors at each table step in to help.]

Small Group Discussion

Mentor: You're struggling? You look like you're struggling.

Youth: So, a challenge would be, like, peer pressure?

Mentor: No, you have to be more specific than that. Take a specific situation, like, Andre and I were in the store and Andre said, "I'm going to steal these cookies." That's a specific situation. And I told Andre, "Why would you steal chocolate chip cookies, they don't even taste that good?" So, we stole red velvet cookies instead. So, be specific like that.

Either think about the situation that brought you here or anything similar. Right now you could just write if you got into a fight or something like that. Then you need to go into details about the choice you made.

Andre: So, like, somebody died?

Mentor: Yeah, something like that.

Andre: Like the death of a friend. I could, like, avenge them?

Mentor: Yes, you're right. So what's the choice here, to avenge the death or not, right? Did you do it?

Andre: No. But I don't know what my outcome is.

Mentor: Well, you didn't avenge your friend's death, so what did you do instead?

Andre: Probably smoked or something.

Mentor: Okay, but what did you do instead? What was the outcome?

Andre: I just went to the gathering they had. The wake, whatever you wanna call it. I hung around with the friends who all came. But I don't know how to explain what I was feeling.

Mentor: You don't have to explain that now. That's the detail for later. So the outcome was, you didn't avenge the death, you went to the gathering instead, right?

Andre: Yeah.

Mentor: Okay, good.

[The mentors turn to the next youth in their small group.]

Mentor: What was your challenge?

Tyrone: I was peer pressured.

Mentor: Into what?

Tyrone: Hittin' a lick.

Mentor: What is "hitting a lick"? Robbing?

Tyrone: Yeah. It's hitting a lick. It's quick. Snap.

Mentor: Spell it.

Tyrone: L-i-c-k. If I call him to hit a lick, I'm gonna say, "Yo, bro, what's good? I got a lick. You down?"

Mentor: Okay, so you *did* the theft?

Tyrone: Yeah.

Mentor: Oh, so you thought about not doing it, but you ended up doing it?

Tyrone: Yeah.

Mentor: So your choice was to do it. You went against your intuition and did it. That's all you need to say right now.

[Time is up for part one and the moderator steps back in.]

Laura, Large Group Discussion

Everybody, let me get your attention. So now, even if you haven't fully written it out yet, share your situation with your group at your table. The challenge, choice, outcome, and lesson. As a small group, you guys will start adding details.

As you tell them what you wrote, the rest of your group is going to ask you for more of the story. More details. I need the mentors to pose questions.

One story might be, "I was about to get into a fight over a bag of chips." What's one question that we could ask?

[The youth offer their potential questions.]

Why you fighting over a bag of chips?

What kind of chips were they?

What size was the bag?

Who were you fighting with?

Where was the fight about to occur?

What time of day was it?

How big was the other kid? That's *very* relevant!

Colleen

A round of laughter interrupts the brainstorming and brings welcomed comic relief. The boys have deep, chilling stories.

Their individual histories are muddled with more obstacles and setbacks than most people will ever know.

Sometimes a little humor in our groups cuts through the outer shell in order to heal the bruised, soft center hiding inside.

• • •

CHAPTER 33

After identifying their defining moment of a challenge, the boys needed to add the details that would make their stories come alive. Each small group huddled at their table and dug into the assignment.

Small Group Discussion

Mentor: So, pull out the details in the stories. One person is speaking, everyone else is listening. Andre, you might as well go first.

Andre: You want me to tell you what I put? My challenge was the death of childhood friends.

Mentor: But in this case, pick one example.

Andre: Probably the most recent one is my homegirl, Jaz. [33] She died Dec 2, 2015. Her name was Jazmine. She went by Jaz.

Mentor: So, write this down, we're building your story. Write her name down. What did she look like?

[Andre points to the button pinned to his shirt in Jaz's honor. The young woman's dark face was lit with a brilliant smile. A date marked her last day of life.]

Andre: She was gay, so she wanted to be like a boy.

Mentor: But describe her. You can describe her personality.

Andre: If you ask me, she was nice, big hearted . . .

Mentor: Was she one to make jokes or one to laugh at them?

Andre: She'd be laughing, I'd say she was goofy.

---

[33] All names in Andre's story are changed to protect the privacy of the family.

Mentor: How long did you know her?

Andre: Since sixth grade.

Mentor: How old was she?

Andre: She was nineteen when she passed.

Mentor: What do you miss most about her?

Andre: Sometimes when my grandmother's house gets hot, like, I could slide on her.[34]

Mentor: Because she had A/C?

Andre: Yeah.

[Laughter surrounds the table.]

Mentor: I know that feeling, because I didn't have A/C growing up either, so I know exactly what you're talking about!

Andre: What else do I miss? It's a *lot*. Just her personality, how she was. I just think she ain't deserve that.

Mentor: What she got?

Andre: Yeah.

Mentor: What's your last memory of her?

Andre: Last time I saw her, she threw a party for her girlfriend's son. Three days later, she died.

Mentor: How did she pass away?

Andre: She got shot five times.

Mentor: Were they aiming for her or was it a fluke?

Andre: She was the only one outside and she got shot five times. One in the head. It was in Atapata, but I don't remember the street name. In a neighborhood called Bataie.

Mentor: Why do they call it Bataie?

Andre: That ain't my hood! That's just what they call it! I just know they normally speak Spanish over there.

Mentor: So, the challenge, you said, was to avenge her death, right?

Andre: Yeah.

---

[34] That is, go over to her house.

Mentor: So what was your choice?

Andre: The challenge was that I'm good friends with her girlfriend, and she kept coming back to me saying stuff—you know how they say the streets talk? She kept telling me and my other homeboys that some of them finna slide.

Mentor: I don't know what slide means.

Andre: Okay, so I said I was friends with her girlfriend and she was saying names of possible suspects. So we go off on them leads and pay them a visit. That means we gonna do revenge, basically. I had to make a choice . . . I didn't do it, but it ain't that I didn't want to.

Mentor: Did you imagine doing it?

Andre: Yeah.

Mentor: Could you see yourself doing it?

Andre: Yeah.

Mentor: What would you have liked to do?

Andre: Slide.

Mentor: But what did you imagine doing? You were going to shoot them?

Andre: Yeah. Standing over him. Shooting him in the head. So, when we was talking about it and stuff, we planned it.

Mentor: What was the plan?

Andre: The plan was, one of her uncles got plugs,[35] so he was gonna give us the guns and one of my homeboys was gonna steal a car. He wasn't gonna go with us, but he was gonna steal the car for us. Four of us was gonna go. One person to stay in the car, and me and the other two was gonna get out and walk and just go do it and run back to the car on the next block.

Mentor: You had the whole thing planned out?

Andre: Yeah.

Mentor: So why did you make the choice not to do it?

---

[35] That is, guns.

Andre: The reason I really ain't do it is cuz we ain't know it for sure. I wanted to know for sure cuz I ain't wanna hop on the news and then find out we did the wrong thing. It seemed pretty believable. That's why I was like, I'm ready.

Mentor: Do you think it was true, that they were right about who did it?

Andre: I think it's still true cuz the boy who they was saying did it, he stays in that area where she died. So I'd be going over there, dropping a teddy bear or lighting candles. I don't smoke weed no more, but I'd go over there and smoke a black[36] and chill for a minute, and I seen the fool. He came one day when I was over there and he was talking to me and acting weird. That's when I was like, I think this nigger did it. You know, he looked like he was scared.

Mentor: Based on what?

Andre: How he was acting and the type of questions he was asking. He was, like, shady.

Mentor: What was his motive?

Andre: I ain't gonna lie. My homegirl, Jaz . . . I ain't gonna say she was a pimp but she had a lot of females over there. There was a particular girl she was dealing with, she used to bring my homegirl weed and get her money and stuff. So I guess fool was trying to put down that the girl was his, and he was trying to tell my homegirl how he ain't gonna have that girl hanging with us and stuff. My homegirl Jaz is like, "She's with us cuz she wants to be." So they got into it. They say he got real mad cuz the girl was on drugs and he was like, "I ain't gonna let this black-eyed hoe be trying my shit." They think the girl was loyal to him and set Jaz up, cuz what was supposed to be happening was Jaz was supposed to be going outside to get some keys from the girl and when Jaz went outside, she was shot when she got to the front

---

[36] That is, clove cigarette.

gate. . . . What makes it so funny, she was on the phone with her girlfriend, her real girlfriend; they say the other girl was a side piece. Her girlfriend heard everything on the phone, and right before she died, Jaz said, "Hold on," and her girlfriend heard a loud horn beep, then she heard a shot and a scream and the phone went dead.

Another youth: So the police ain't got nobody?

Andre: No, at first they grabbed him and they grabbed her, but they let them both go.

Mentor: Since you still think he did it, do you still think about, you know, still getting revenge?

[A dark silence fell.]

Andre: Yeah. Only when I see him and I start thinking about it. And I think, I don't know, I just think this nigger did it.

Mentor: So, let's say you got the revenge. Imagine that you did it. What do you think you'd get from it? In real life. For real. Aside from the satisfaction of knowing the person is dead? And if you think about it, everyone's going to die, so he *is* going to die. So, besides your satisfaction of making him meet his death earlier, what would you get from it? Cuz it ain't gonna bring her back.

Andre: I mean it's just how he done killed Jaz. That was it. It ain't really about getting something back. I don't know what you mean.

Mentor: Okay, how about this . . . In your opinion, what do you think is the best way to let her memory live on? Do you think revenge is the best way or just honoring her memory, like you're doing on your shirt right now? Maybe checking in on her peeps every now and then?

Andre: I thought revenge was a better way. Sometimes I still do, that's what I'm saying. I can still do it cuz I know where he be.

Mentor: So let me ask you this, when you think that it's the best way, are you typically angry and pissed off?

Andre: I think about it when I start reminiscing. That's when it comes on my mind and I just be like, that was fucked up.

Mentor: I try my best not to make decisions when I'm too much of anything. If I'm too happy, I don't want to make a decision because I'm not really thinking straight because I'm so happy and excited. If I'm too pissed off, I don't make decisions either because now I'm acting off of anger. I try to make decisions when I'm cool. Right now you seem like you're in a cool, calm state of mind where you can think intellectually. So sitting here right now, do you think it would be a good decision?

Andre: Naw.

Mentor: So the only thing I can impart on you is that any time you're feeling like that, be like, You know, I'm not going to make a decision while I'm hot right now, while I'm reminiscing. Let me cool it off for a minute. There's a lot of dudes sitting behind bars that made decisions while pissed off. Then they'd be saying I can't even live for that person the way I wanted to because how're you going to do that from behind bars?

Another Mentor: That's a good point, because if you were to avenge her death and get locked up, you won't be able to do the small things you do for her family. When you make a decision, you have to keep in mind that you're not only making the decision for you, you're making the decision for your family, the people who care about you, and there are people rooting for you and as hard as it may be to know who did it and not take action, you have to realize there's a better way of solving that problem. You can't bring her back. And you can't retaliate for everyone you lost. At some point, maybe you can realize you can make different decisions and surround yourself with different people. Not that she was a bad person, but you don't want to keep yourself in a dangerous environment with people whose lives are always threatened. You're going to be forced to make these decisions and have these thoughts all the time.

You lose her and then you lose somebody next month, and the month after. Do you avenge them, too? At some point, you have to separate that and be like, 'No. This is not how I handle a situation. This isn't the right thing to do.'

So what was the outcome? I know one outcome. You're sitting with us today!

Mentor: Seriously!

[Relief finally sweeps over the table and the mentors start to ease back into their seats after the intense discussion.]

Mentor: I do want to say I'm proud that you decided not to go through with revenge.

Another mentor: Yeah, it takes a lot of self-respect not to act.

Mentor: I'm definitely proud you could share the story and even tell us you were considering that. You got "Blessed" on your arm, so I know you believe in something. I can tell you that no higher power would say, "Go kill somebody," no matter who your higher power is.

Another mentor: So what's the lesson?

Andre: The lesson was—and I prayed on this— everything happens for a reason, that's what I came to.

Mentor: Do you believe it?

Andre: Yeah.

Mentor: Can you give us a reason?

Andre: What?

Mentor: One of the reasons for that situation.

Andre: Well, Jaz's little brother's named Bean. She would always talk about him a lot, because he got shot in the head before and he almost died. So she was always like, Bean, Bean,

Bean. Then when she died, he hollered[37] at me cuz he knew me and her was close. I ain't gonna lie, he said he wanted to smoke and all that. I gave him some weed and we smoked. That's when Jaz first died. He was just talking and all that. So now I took her shoes[38] a little bit, not a lot. Cuz he hits me up when he wants to and he ain't have to do that. When it first happened, he was quiet.

Mentor: You can look at it as a motivation for you to do better as well. Because you can easily go back to what you know, because you're surrounded by it. Think about it, you're in this program because you committed a crime and you're getting positive reinforcement here every week that there's more to life. And then you have this happen to you. Prior to what you've experienced with Empowered Youth, do you think you would have made the right decision?

Andre: Oh! Naw.

Mentor: So everything does happen for a reason!

Another mentor: You better start writing down some of that detail, my friend. Who wants to go next?

Colleen

This cathartic exercise repeats time and time again. In many forums, with various activities, with different youth and mentors, and with any topic. Somehow, simple exercises open giant floodgates and allow enlightenment, understanding, friendship, healing, and growth to take hold.

---

[37] That is, hollered at, or called.
[38] That is, took her shoes, or filled in for her.

CHAPTER 34

When I see the boys' progress and their active participation in the program, it melts me. I wish society could see how most of these boys want to do the right thing. Understandably, they're often judged on their rap sheet, but I feel people will be most open and accepting of them if they are pleasant, thoughtful, and polite. Therefore, ingraining manners is a specific goal.

A poster that we place outside the truck while we work explains the premise and goal of Empowered Youth. Many passersby love the concept and stop to talk to us, even as we're prepping before the opening.

"Oh, you guys have all been in trouble before? Wow, this is good! What time do you open?" they might say. Or sometimes, "Wow, you're the only nonprofit food truck! Do you guys have flyers?" The public response is genuinely supportive and the polished behavior of the boys doesn't go unnoticed.

Many of the thank-you notes I receive after events are complimentary of both the food and the behavior of the boys. "They were very polite and everybody was smiling," they often say.

Many indicators convince me we're on the right path: from the results I see with the boys, to their rapt engagement in the culinary process, to the jobs that can be a springboard for future employment elsewhere. Besides the benefit to the boys, we're providing a service that the community needs, enjoys, and appreciates.

If I had finally honed a winning formula, how could I expand the model to make a bigger impact? To help more boys? To provide more opportunities? As a further extension of the functioning hospitality model, I envisioned the Vibe 305 Culinary Training Center & Café.

The Vibe 305 food truck would continue gigs at various venues, while the training center and café would house the kitchen and other services we currently borrow from Trinity Cathedral for our culinary classes. I visualized a "farm to table" café concept, stemming from a large onsite garden that would be planted, tended, and harvested by the boys. The fresh produce would supply both the café kitchen and the food truck.

Another fringe benefit of having the boys involved in growing the food would be their exposure to the full spectrum of the culinary process—from gardening awareness to learning how to eat well and feed a family.

By my calculation, the envisioned café could employ fifty youth. It would be fifty jobs I desperately needed for the boys and for income to keep the program afloat.

I committed my pipe dream to paper, and once I'd documented the plan, I went in search of the ever-elusive funding that could bring my new vision to life.

At this point, I'd accrued plenty of networking experience and creative ways to keep inching forward. Once again, I hit the streets with pleas for help and a miraculous windfall landed in my lap. A parcel of prime real estate, nestled in the desirable Wynwood Yard Art District, would become the site of our future center.

Ana Marie Beebe and Deena Bell Llewellyn are angels who worked pro bono for more than two years as our building and landscape architects, respectively. They laid out the facility and grounds that included a café, a container for an educational center, a garden, and a stage for musical performances.

Stubborn determination chips away at the many pieces of this project. I'm certain my vision will come to life. The only question is when.

Beyond the café and culinary center, my master plan also includes expansion of the EY Neighborhood Program into more communities. Our current hub is Liberty City, where we've met the extent of our geographic reach. My planned expansion into other inner-city communities is ready and waiting for funding.

Another aspect of the program will be enacted with the launch of the Vibe 305 Culinary Training Center & Café. Young men who successfully complete the program would be eligible for a scholarship to pursue some additional training or education, whether it be an extension into a culinary arts program, a college degree, or a vocational school. Even if they secure other scholarships, there's always an assortment of other costs, such as books and housing. I look forward to the day when we're profitable enough to offer this additional path to a brighter future.

My plans run five steps ahead of my funding. Not only does reaching so far forward keep me aiming for the stars, but it ensures any donation dollars are put to their best use, and the impact to my beloved boys and their communities is maximized.

CHAPTER 35

No child asks to be born and no child asks to be born into poverty, abuse, or abandonment. But for the last eleven years, I've seen the result of this American tragedy firsthand, even while waiting in a courtroom for my kids' cases to be called.

A scene I watch too often is that of a young teenager, in court for some offense, and his mother is sitting nearby, twitching in a way I've come to recognize is the result of drug use. She's unwittingly training her child to be a criminal, grooming him for a life in the system.

I see these kids' futures falling apart, beginning in the home. Our goal is to break this cycle for each boy currently in the program, which totals about twenty-five boys at any given time.

One beautiful benefit of our program is giving the boys a glimpse of a family they might not otherwise experience. The Empowered Youth birthday and Christmas celebrations may be the only ones the youth ever have.

But we're like any family. We may stumble and scrape our knees sometimes, but we always stay in the race. My journey with each young man who enters the program is different. Each travels his own path in his own time. I plant the seeds but the rest is up to them. Even a boy who chooses to leave the program carries the seeds we've planted within him. They may sprout in prison or elsewhere, but at some point, an alternative idea has been implanted in the psyche of that young person. That's why I don't use the word "failure," because the seeds we plant have varying degrees of success, just like in nature.

Sometimes the boys cycle out of the program because they lose their temper, they don't know how to accept instructions, or they simply aren't ready to change. Each person has to make the choice for himself to change.

I can't beat myself up over the losses, although I have moments of great sadness and disappointment. I've cried many times because it's sad to lose a kid I love back to the system or to his environment.

At the same time I have great resilience about it, because the long line of at-risk youth is wrapping around the building. Those kids are who inspire and motivate me, just like my spilled creamer philosophy: I did my best, but this adverse outcome happened. I can't turn it back, so my only option is to move forward.

I used to feel hurt when someone left the program or was asked to leave, but I've come to accept any outcome, because these kids face situations and pressures that I can't even imagine. I used to take it as a reflection on me, but at the end of the day it's really about the boys. I do my best and they have to do their best, but sometimes those two don't meet in the middle. There've been kids I really thought would do well and make it and some of them have and some haven't.

But I'm certain that seeds are planted when a child like Andre says, "The program showed me that life ain't just the hood. I can do stuff and learn something and by me learning that one thing, it can take me a lot of places and I can meet a lot of people. Before the program, my world was small. It was just the city and everything else I know. That was it. Now I have dreams. If I ever make it, like to make millions, I want to start a center, like an outreach. An outlet for kids in the hood."

I can't always predict the outcomes, but our track record proves the overall success of the program. The great majority of Empowered Youth students navigate their way out of the abyss with some guidance, patience, training, and opportunity.

Let's take Demetrius[39] as one example. When he first came to the program, oh my goodness! He was loud and boisterous, behaving completely out of control on so many nights. I would take that kid home and say, "Demetrius, dude. You're not going to make it if you just can't control yourself."

Although he was a talented athlete, his sassy mouth and attitude got him kicked off many football teams, which he was hoping would be his ticket out of the hood. I eventually helped him get on a football team through a contact I had. Demetrius later texted me that he's going to California to play football, news that gave me chills. He was one of those kids you'd never imagine could turn it around, but he did.

Then I have those bright stars like Juan. This young man has transcended an extremely challenging upbringing and shines in any leadership role he's offered, from a lead role on the food truck to public speaking at various engagements. Juan is one of our students in progress and I can already see his seeds are sprouting into beautiful flowers.

When Todd Bass inquired if I had an Empowered Youth graduate who would like to serve on the Circuit Advisory Board, I immediately considered Juan. Not only had he performed outstanding in the program, but his interest in criminal justice made him a perfect fit and I was pleased to nominate him:

> My name is Colleen Adams [. . .] and I am nominating a graduate of my program, Juan [last name] for the position of Youth Representative for the Circuit Advisory Board.

> Juan has been with the Empowered Youth Program for almost three years and has served in many capacities during that timeframe.

---

[39] Name has been changed to respect the privacy of the family.

Juan was court-referred to my program when he was fifteen years old and has never looked back. During his tenure with Empowered Youth, Juan represented the program at the Global Homeboy Conference in Los Angeles (where he spoke before an assembly of international participants); at the White House in Washington, D.C.; and also represented the program at a youth leadership conference in Costa Rica.

Juan began training in the Empowered Youth Job Development Program when he graduated from the program, and has since been promoted to the Assistant to the Chef on the food truck, and will be a Management Trainee at the Vibe 305 Culinary Training Center & Café in Wynwood.

When Juan entered the program, his GPA was 1.9; and he graduated from Miami Springs High School this past June with a GPA of 2.5. Juan is currently waiting for his financial aid to be approved so he can start college at Miami-Dade College, where he will major in criminal justice and work as a juvenile probation officer to help other young men like himself.

All of these accomplishments by a young man marked for failure three years ago. Dogged by poverty and surrounded by crime, Juan had the strength of character to rise above those challenges and become a hero to his younger brothers, a provider for his family, and a leader in his community. All at age eighteen.

I submit that there could be no better youth representative for your Circuit Advisory Board than Juan [last name]. He represents the outcome of what can happen when we believe and invest in our inner-city young men.

Juan was accepted to the Advisory Board, adding a beneficial perspective to the other board members and a valuable line item to his impressive and expanding résumé.

Vondell[40] is another current student creating a brighter future, no matter the numerous challenges of his past. His upbringing came straight from the broken mold, with career criminals as his role models, yet it never dampened his forgiving and loving spirit.

He and his girlfriend became teen parents to a beautiful baby girl, but they struggle without positive examples of a functional couple. History is begging to repeat itself.

Despite the mountain of obstacles threatening to hold him down, Vondell hasn't veered from the right path. Although high ground evades him, he keeps his head above a rising tide using a constant doggie paddle. His determination and willingness to work as opposed to illegal means of income is a choice. He'd been conditioned his whole life to take unlawful shortcuts and end up in prison. Despite that, he's chosen to work on the food truck, earning an honest living for his daughter and family, demonstrating his commendable strength, resilience, and resolve.

Deon is another example of a young man who's fighting with everything he has to make a new life for himself.

---

[40] Name has been changed to respect the privacy of the family.

Deon, EY Student

I was a troubled youth and was court-ordered to Empowered Youth. Once I started going, I liked it a lot. We have talk sessions where we sit in a group and talk about everything that's happening. It's a pretty good group.

When I first came, Miss Colleen said she had a food truck, and my biggest struggle had been finding a job. She put me on the truck and ever since then, I've been doing what I'm supposed to do and working on the truck. I'm making money for my family and helping them, with all the problems they have. Everything's been going good, and I've been staying out of trouble.

It wasn't hard when I first came because all I had to do was just sit down and listen to what they were talking about. I was glad to be there. I'd heard about it from people I knew and they said it was good. So I was kind of happy when I got court-ordered there.

The UM student mentors help me because anything I have a problem with, like reading or math, they teach me how to do it and make it easier for me to solve problems, or anything I need help with. We talk about our problems and they give good advice, and we give them good advice back!

Empowered Youth changed me by giving me advice almost every day. It's good information to put in my head so I don't go back out there robbing people and stealing things to get locked back up. Now that I have a job and I'm keeping it, it's going very well. I don't have to worry about how I'm going to get money anymore.

I'm working on my GED now and hope to have it in the next six months, then I plan to go to school for a trade, maybe air-conditioning repair, which is needed in Miami.

Empowered Youth has also helped because if my plan for A/C doesn't work out, I have experience as a chef, so I could go to culinary arts school. But everything is really working out for me now. I've been staying out of a lot of trouble. I got a couple of homeboys that I grew up with and they still hang around me but I just sit there and tell them the good information they should know, like they shouldn't be going out doing the crazy stuff they do and they should get a job. Of course, they gonna do what they do, but it's good that I'm staying out of it.

All the Empowered Youth staff are helpful and give good information or help you with anything you need. If you have any problem, you can go to any of them, especially Miss Colleen. She'll try to help you the best way she can. I appreciate them a lot. It's a good support system for anybody. If you really want to change, it will help you change. I've been in the program almost nine months now and I'm proud of the changes I've made.

Colleen

Then there's Jamal.[41] At the time he was in the program, Jamal was assigned a mentor who took him places and expanded his view of what the world held outside the hood. He did well in the program and eventually ended up as a mentor himself. We were in the process of launching a clothing line and Jamal found that he enjoyed the sales aspect and how it easy it was for him to talk to people. "Hey, this is EY, come buy a shirt from us!" he'd call out to draw in potential customers.

Jamal hailed from circumstances beyond comprehension of mainstream America, yet he successfully completed the program and forged his path out of poverty. He showed ambition to do more and be more, but he struggled to break apart from his roots that seemed to keep him bound.

---

[41] Name has been changed to respect the privacy of the family.

He accomplished the separation he needed by joining the Army Airborne Infantry Division, which stationed him in Alaska. After his discharge, he became a car salesman, then applied and was accepted into the police academy. After he completes the six-month program, he plans to become a police officer.

Jamal is just one of our amazing successes. He's hopeful that his story can inspire others who come from challenging circumstances.

Jamal, Former EY Student

I want to tell people [from the hood] to keep pushing even though it may seem hard. Everything I did was pretty hard, but I still did it. I came from the worst. I lived in a house with twenty-two people with three bedrooms and one bathroom. But I still made it. I stayed in the projects and saw my friend get shot in the back six times. But I can't let that or the people around me define me. I made my own destiny.

Your destiny isn't set in stone. You're in charge of your own fate. You plan your own future and you decide what you want to do with your life. If you work hard enough to reach a goal, there's nothing in this world that can stop you. The only one who can stop you is *you.*

I had every excuse in the world that you could have. But if you try hard and really want it, go get it. So instead of thinking, I can't do it because of this or that, there's always a way of doing things. You just have to find it.

Colleen

I've had countless men who've graduated and go on to work at local hotels and restaurants and each are a success in their own right. I've learned you just have to keep sticking with these young men like no one's ever done before.

I'm proud of the accomplishments of many of the students, but I'm especially gratified to see young men overcome such overwhelming odds and turn their lives around completely. Maurice[42] is another example.

Maurice, Former EY Student

I joined Empowered Youth in 2009. My older brother was in the program, so I came with him and I liked it.

I wasn't really an at-risk child. I was a good student, I just didn't like the neighborhood I was in, and so I wanted to stay away from home as much as possible. I never wanted to be like everybody else around me, I wanted to be different. A lot of my friends ended up dead or in jail and I definitely didn't want to be like that either. Every time we'd go out, my friends would be wearing baggy jeans and flashy shoes, and I'd be the one in a button-down shirt with some slacks and some kicks. I was that type of guy: the different one.

The program exposed me to a lot of situations that helped me. We started a T-shirt line while I was there. I wrote the essay to designer Kenneth Cole so we could get it started. It didn't boom as we expected, but it was one of the money-making things that helped me and kept me out of trouble. We later started the food truck.

I became a mentor to the Empowered Youth students after I graduated. I was in the program during the first cycle of boys and I think they're on the eighth or ninth cycle now. I don't think I've ever seen a more troubled group of teenagers than those we're getting today. Miss Colleen may not be able to change

---

[42] Name has been changed to respect the privacy of the family.

them all, but each time, she changes at least 95 percent of them. Miss Colleen Adams, she sure knows how to do her job well.

As for myself, I used to be a hoodlum out in the street and now I'm doing something with my life. Miss Colleen encouraged me to get out and try new things. I was a quiet, solitary guy and didn't like talking to people. Now I'm a great public speaker—things like that. I'm grateful for everything she's done for me.

Right now, I'm currently in the Marine Corps. I'm married and have a couple of kids. I'm doing great and I can't say I'd be this far without her. Because of Miss Colleen, I ended up getting an internship at the Biltmore Hotel in Coral Gables as a chef and then they hired me. It was my first official job and I made good money there. Then I joined the Marine Corps, and later came back to Miami. Colleen has a way of making you feel welcome no matter what. Every time I came home, there was always a place for me at Empowered Youth.

I come to the program as much as I can. With a family, it's pretty hard. When I'm there, I do my best to keep order in the meetings, give advice, and take a leadership role on Saturday field trips. I try to build a friendly relationship with the students so they don't feel like I'm just over their heads all the time, pushing them. I believe in positive reinforcement, that when you give "great," you get "great" in return. That's what I try to implement with the students.

I definitely recommend this program to both mentors and youth. To potential mentors who want to help, but are afraid, I say, "Don't be." I had to think about the safety aspect, too, when I became a mentor. The boys are just like you when you were younger. They're not bad kids, they were brought up in a bad situation, and you do have to have a lot of patience to become a mentor in the program.

And to the youth, I say, "Give the program a chance." Trust me when I say, I had to give it a chance, too. Sitting in a circle talking about your problems is not something that everybody wants to do. A lot of boys may come in with the attitude of "that damn white lady," but you have to put yourself out there. You'll meet new people and establish new connections and other things that are uncomfortable at first, but give it a chance.

Colleen

Maurice overcame his slim odds and entered the army, where he specialized in information technology and is now attending college. He's married with a step-child he's raising as his own, along with their new baby. It may seem like any typical American family, but marriage and commitment aren't typical in the hood. Yet Maurice did the right thing to have the family he always craved.

I can't fix poverty, crime, or the breakdown of American families. But I'm aiming to establish a perpetual path out of inner-city poverty, one that provides a light for the lost, for generations to come. My dream is to hand off a sustainable process to a dedicated young man who's willing to maintain the momentum. Will that be Juan? Andre? Hakim or Fernando? Or maybe someone I haven't met yet. There's one thing for certain: As long as I'm able, I'm going to show these boys a better way. I fully anticipate and desire to exit this world while doing this work that I love with the students I love.

CHAPTER 36

I've learned more in this last decade than I ever imagined. One tough lesson has been the difficulty of getting the program funded. It's been a long road, but we're still relatively young and growing. I see and feel the momentum rising as the Vibe 305 brand catches on.

Most notable is the materialization of our Vibe 305 Culinary Training Center & Café project, due to spring to life in 2017. Thanks to the incredible generosity of supportive partners, plus innumerable sweat-equity hours and sleepless nights, the project will no longer be a static set of blueprints, but a brand-new three-dimensional live phase of the program that will allow me to help the boys exponentially. This addition will provide training, jobs, and a positive future for up to fifty inner-city young men. The culinary training center and café will be the final step in our "Street to Success" pipeline and will allow our students to step into the real world of work and entrepreneurship prepared for success!

Outstanding restaurant expertise and leadership will be provided by Chef Ronnie, executive sous chef at Joe's Stone Crab restaurant for the past fifteen years. A partnership with the Florida Restaurant & Lodging Association (FRLA) will ensure the training of our students in all of the technical, front-of-the-office/house, and customer service skills needed to work successfully in the hospitality industry. In addition, the FRLA will conduct a job fair for our graduates that will allow them to obtain permanent jobs in the hospitality industry.

I'm overjoyed and hopeful that this next phase of the program will provide another stepping stone to our franchise model that could be expanded to assist inner-city youth in major cities across America.

The results speak for themselves. Ninety-four percent of the participants of the Vibe 305 Food Truck Job Development Program have not reoffended. This success is building our reputation, which is vital to attract the people, supporters, and donors who could help us achieve the franchise model.

People can now see the boys are making it. Program graduates are working in the community. We've developed an impressive track record and amassed a lengthy list of wins, proving the program works. It has taken years to build trust and earn credibility with the public, but at this point, people are starting to think I might be on to something.

Our biggest challenge is always funding, because many people wouldn't consider these kids a "good investment." But I know better.

I'm blessed to work with these young people. I've never worked harder and I've never been poorer, but what would I do differently? Nothing. I can't turn away, knowing these kids have no voice and no one to fight for them or stand with them. How can you put a value or price on life?

I used to have a comfortable lifestyle. Now my clothes are well used and a vacation is just a pleasant memory. Those things erode you spiritually after a while, not to mention the stress of shaky financial footing.

I'm still as human as they come. I can be ornery, impatient, and a confounded perfectionist. I make many mistakes and hurt people's feelings with brutal honesty, even with the purest intention.

Sometimes I gaze out over the inviting ocean and imagine sipping Chardonnay with my girlfriends somewhere, maybe on a sailing adventure to the Galapagos Islands. I fantasize about having that lifestyle again for five minutes.

I may not be nominated for sainthood, but I do understand kindness, compassion, empathy, determination, commitment, justice, and faith. I work hard to be a good person, honest, kind, and forgiving. I lead with an open heart that has room for as many kids as I can fit into it and with enough love to feed the souls of as many people as I can touch. I love easily and forgive easily and always lead with empathy. I'm not perfect, but I strive to work in the image of a loving God who views all of His children with tenderness and forgiveness.

Because what is the point of life really? Is it only supposed to be about my creature comfort, or is it supposed to be about using what I know and who I am to try to move the ball a bit forward for humanity?

When I lay my weary body onto my welcoming bed each night, I know I gave my best, no matter what transpired that day.

One of my kids who graduated five years ago called me recently.

"Miss Colleen, it's Eddie. I've been looking everywhere for you," he said.

"Oh, Eddie, I'm so happy to hear from you! How are you?"

"Oh, Miss Colleen, you're the only person who can help me. I relapsed. Can you help me? Can you talk to me? You're the only one I can talk to about this."

Even though I was sad to hear this, it was both rewarding and wonderful to know that this young man had someone to reach out to in his dark moment.

I told him, "Thank you for reaching out to me. I'm honored you thought I would be able to help you."

It's kids like Eddie and Maurice and Juan and Jamal and hundreds of others that keep me motivated.

My life's work with inner-city youth has been a culmination of everything I've ever experienced: every great moment I've had, every professional accomplishment, and every skill I've learned. Each one is applied to the program and helping my kids. Whether it's organizational skills, marketing, or writing, all are laser-focused on creating a better life for a bunch of kids who really don't have a chance otherwise.

Has this mission been hard? Absolutely. But any discouragement or disheartenment hasn't been caused by the kids, but instead by their community that doesn't support them.

I remind myself of the saying that "a journey of a thousand miles begins with one step." When I consider my life's work in that way, I don't get fatigued, because each day the journey renews with a fresh start.

I know with certainty my life could be so much easier and stress-free. I try to reconcile that with the three hours I spend crawling through city traffic to pick up kids from some of the most dangerous neighborhoods in the country, running them back and forth to the program, and the endless fights to try to change their thinking and their choices. But as draining, frustrating, and relentless as this work can be, it sustains me in the most fundamental way.

Many years ago I took the "tombstone test" as I wallowed on my living room floor, lost and confused as to my life's path. Since those dark days, I've strived to live my life worthy of two words etched in stone:

She cared.

Epilogue

Todd Bass, Miami-Dade State Attorney's Office:
Juvenile Division

People who live in high-crime inner-city neighborhoods recognize that juvenile delinquency is a problem. But even if you're not from those neighborhoods, we're all still affected by kids who are on the pathway to incarceration.

Armed robbery is a first-degree felony, punishable by up to life in prison, likely without parole. You can make a deal, and maybe end up with less time, but mostly it's life in prison.

There's no question that in America we incarcerate more people than any other country in the world. Some people must be incarcerated because their crimes are heinous. But for lesser crimes, society, as a whole, could benefit by not having the additional costs of lifetime incarceration.

An amazing amount of money—billions of taxpayer dollars—is spent incarcerating people for life. The cost of the juvenile justice system isn't cheap either, and it varies from state to state. Clearly, alternative programs that stem the tide of crime and reduce costly incarceration are in the best interest of society.

In Florida, prosecutors have 100 percent discretion on most cases as to whether a juvenile will be sent to adult court, but that has to be used the right way. We use it as a last resort. If a juvenile commits a heinous crime, such as taking a gun to someone and demanding their property, that's something that can terrorize the victim for life, depending on how they deal with sensitivities and emotions. If the offender is sixteen or seventeen years old, that's a mandatory direct file, which means they must go into the adult process. So we have to reach those kids one step before they get to that point, and get them into programs like Empowered Youth.

We have serious gang violence out there, so we need an alternative. We need to occupy the juveniles' time with worthwhile projects, whatever that is, be it sports or other opportunities to make some money the right way, like Empowered Youth provides. We have to reach more kids earlier, before they get too far off track.

We need the Empowered Youth program to grow because there are kids who could have been saved if we'd gotten them into programs like this sooner. Why would anyone want to deal with the fear and violence involved with a gang if they have a group of people they love and who want them to be successful?

To become eligible for the Empowered Youth program, the offending juvenile takes a plea in court. So, it's a done deal, with the provision that they must successfully complete the program. Colleen determines when they have successfully completed it, because some kids come around more quickly than others and Colleen knows that. One young man might need six months, but another might need eight months, or even a year. When the juvenile completes the program to Colleen's satisfaction, his charges are vacated and dismissed.

It's a carrot-and-stick program. It's a great reward for the effort needed. If they've done too serious a charge, they're not even eligible. Armed robbery? No way. We're not dismissing an armed robbery just because someone does a program. We're very sensitive to the victims' concerns, needs, and issues.

There are few programs like Empowered Youth that can really stem the tide of crime. That's why this program needs to expand. There are other mentoring programs that might make a child feel good right then and there, but they don't necessarily help them for jobs and money. We have kids who aren't going on to higher education, so we have to provide them some alternative, because what else are they going to do? Empowered Youth gives them training and knowledge for a future.

A lot of times there has to be tough love, too. My original concern was that we'd send Colleen referrals, but if that kid wasn't holding up his end of the deal, would she bounce him out and let us know? I was never certain, because this is the land of second and third chances. But when a kid has crossed the boundary with her, she knows she's not helping them if she just lets it slide.

People in the judicial system are just trying to do their job, like a defense attorney who fights to get a kid off a charge at any cost. That's his job, but it's not necessarily the best thing for the juvenile because it removes him from a system that would otherwise be helping him.

I would hope every judge, prosecutor, and defense attorney wants to do what's best for the juvenile, but we also need to do what's best for the public. I have to safeguard the public from a dangerous juvenile.

The key is getting a child to believe in himself. Unfortunately, we have kids who don't live for anything and they just don't care anymore. That's a dangerous attitude. A kid who doesn't care might either hurt someone or hurt himself. So you teach them to believe in themselves, to rise above their situation instead of blaming everything *on* their situation. Colleen sets the expectation that they are to rise above their circumstances.

We need people like Colleen who will give unconditional love to these kids because that's what's necessary. These are her kids, literally. It's obvious when you see her around them. She does what she has to do and I love seeing her interacting with the boys because her formula is so successful. You can see it working.

I love seeing the success stories. There are bound to be failures, since ultimately the boys are making their own decisions. But the vast majority of the Empowered Youth kids stay out of trouble and go on to do more with their lives.

Sometimes you see the success years later when they're doing something that they ultimately wouldn't have done. You see the boys reaching plateaus they would have never reached without being in the program. There are kids with jobs, those who've gone on to college, gone into the military, or to other opportunities they wouldn't have done without Colleen's motivation and encouragement.

The food truck is a great opportunity, and the planned restaurant will allow Colleen to employ even more kids and get them off the street. But programs like Empowered Youth have a constant battle for funding.

I would love to see the restaurant open and provide jobs and opportunity for the kids. Besides restaurant jobs, it would give Colleen a way to showcase the boys' multiple talents in art and music.

Sometimes I don't even know how Colleen has survived. She has incredible will, that's the thing. But financially they [Empowered Youth] provide so much for the kids, like food and so many other things, that I don't see how it's possible.

When I first met Colleen in 2008, I was impressed that someone who had such a high level job at Perry Ellis was trying to help the kids. Knowing her as I do now, it would have been clear that her day job wasn't going to last. She has such a passion for something as wonderful as this, and even though there isn't anything wrong with the world of fashion, they're not saving lives like Colleen is doing with these boys.

Acknowledgements

Colleen Adams

To every past and present Empowered Youth young man. I remember all of you. You have each taught me the true meaning of love, courage, and perseverance. Together you have taught me so much more than I could have ever taught you. It has been my honor and privilege to know and love you, and to contribute in some small way to your lives. You allowed me to know myself better and have brought me to the pinnacle of what I believe my destiny in this life was meant to be. I was born to know you and to be a part of your life, and I thank you for allowing me to do that. I am proud of each of you, and my wish is that you will continue to be the best that you can be and to turn around and bring my struggling youth with you. Go back to give back. Always remember where you started and that you needed help along the way, and please return that blessing to others with your time, treasure, or talent. Remember how much I believe in you always, and to be GREAT! I love you all!

The first person who inspired me to do this work—and also set the bar very high—was Father Greg Boyle, internationally acclaimed juvenile justice reform leader and founder of Homeboy Industries. His antigang program reenters former gang members in Los Angeles, and sets the tone for leading with compassion worldwide. Father Greg, you set the spiritual standard that I'm still trying to attain. Your determination and commitment has always inspired me and I thank you for your mentorship and support while I was establishing the EY program. One particular interview with Anderson Cooper left a lasting impression on me. He told you, "A lot of people say that your kids take advantage of you." After giving him a quizzical look, you responded, "I give my advantage away." That comment became my benchmark and I try to live up to it every day by knowing that what I give to my students is in the spirit of one human being lending a hand to another human being, without expectations of gratitude or outcome. There is no charge in this world for sunshine or rainbows . . . or hope.

Long ago, I gave Mr. Jerry the dubious title of CFO—chief functioning officer! Jerry, I just could not have made this program work without your commitment and sacrifice and dedication to the program and the boys. My heartfelt thanks for supporting our program intrepidly in every way humanly possible. You're the backbone of the organization and you grease the wheels to make the machine work. I can't overstate my gratitude for your continued care, support, and commitment to the boys and the program. Thank you!

Thank you to Judge Marcia Caballero and Susanna Guzman-Arian, who supported me from the very beginning by providing the glue, support and helping me to establish the foundation of the Empowered Youth that exists today. You remain my rocks until this very day, your devotion to our students and the cause we serve has never wavered.

Sophia Montenegro, chairman of the EY Board, and Carlos Valdes, board member—and both longtime dear friends of Empowered Youth—provide a daily commitment and find ways to make anything we need happen with no funds. Thank you!

To Dave Lawrence, Carlos Martinez, Marie Osborne, and Todd Bass—thank you for your exemplary work to guide and support our inner-city youth and for your participation and support of both the Empowered Youth program and our book project.

To my great personal friend and program supporter, Martina Spolini. Your passion and enthusiasm for social change, coupled with your accomplished marketing expertise, helped us extend the reach of this book project for the best possible outcome. Thank you! Thank you!

Thank you to Ms. Shirley for your countless hours interviewing our students and EY family members and friends to tell the courageous stories of our young men, and to let the world know who they really are.

Trinity Cathedral has supported our program for many years, and generously welcomes us into their kitchen each Monday night for our culinary classes. They help us every year with Christmas presents for the boys . . . they truly live every word of their spiritual doctrine of love and community.

The University of Miami has supported our program in countless ways over the years (thank you Ms. Marni and Ms. Jan).

University of Miami students from all colleges and disciplines tutor our students every Saturday during the semester and have saved many young men from failing and inspired many more to want to attend college! A truly extraordinary group of young people, for whom we are very grateful.

The undertaking of our café and training center is possible with a team of devoted people, most specifically architect Ana Marie Beebe and landscape architect Deena Bell Llewellyn, both of whom have donated their time to this project for almost three years!

Our program mentors, tutors, volunteers, and community supporters are heroes! Know that your efforts are saving and transforming young lives. You've believed in this project when many didn't, so God bless you many times over for keeping the faith in our young men and our program. As these young men grow into adulthood, know that you have made it possible for them to have a life, a career, and a future that doesn't include prison or an early death on the streets.

ACKNOWLEDGEMENTS

Shirley Alarie

Colleen Adams, you are an incredible inspiration. Since the moment we first spoke and I learned about you and Empowered Youth, I've been in awe of what you've accomplished. You are a rare gem and I can't wait to see the continued evolution of Empowered Youth. Thank you for allowing me to tell your story. Godspeed, my friend.

To all the current and past young men of Empowered Youth, especially those I met personally through this project. Thank you for sharing your journey with me and contributing to this book. Your stories are sure to inspire readers the way they inspired me. Stay on the right track and reach back with your hand extended to other young men who need you.

A big thank-you to Mr. Jerry, not only for your support of this project but for your tireless efforts that help both Ms. Colleen and Empowered Youth.

To all the Empowered Youth supporters, especially those who contributed to this project. You make Empowered Youth possible and your work is lifesaving. Thank you for caring about the boys who need love and support to find a better way in life.

To Dave Lawrence, Carlos Martinez, Marie Osborne, and Todd Bass. Your work changes lives on behalf of those without a real voice. Special thanks for sharing your expertise that lent credibility to our book.

I'm blessed to have wonderful people who support my writing career in various ways; as beta readers, creative critics, and special social media cheerleaders. Heartfelt gratitude to Fran Alarie, Cindy Race, Patti Walker, Cheryl Green, Stacy Pace, MaryJo Spencer, Marion Brenon, and Donna Baldwin.

And last, but most important, is my Numero Uno, Fran Alarie. I'm eternally grateful for your boundless love and incredible support. I love you always.

STAY IN TOUCH WITH US!

Thank you for reading **Hope in the Hood**! Your review on Amazon or other forums is extremely valuable to other readers. Please consider taking a few minutes to leave your review.

FOLLOW Empowered Youth USA: Facebook, Twitter, Instagram, www.empoweredyouthusa.org

CONTACT Colleen Adams: colleen.empoweredyouth@gmail.com

ABOUT THE AUTHOR

A breast cancer diagnosis forced Shirley Alarie to put her life in perspective. Her journey since then has been focused on making a positive difference in the world.

Her Lemons to Lemonade book series serves meaningful and inspirational stories in an engaging way. By increasing awareness of social issues that plague our communities and our world, change becomes possible. **Hope in the Hood** is the third installment of the series. Stay tuned for the next release! "Like" SHIRLEY ALARIE AUTHOR on Facebook or sign up for updates on SHIRLEYALARIE.COM

OTHER BOOKS BY SHIRLEY ALARIE

Lemons to Lemonade Series:
Installment 1

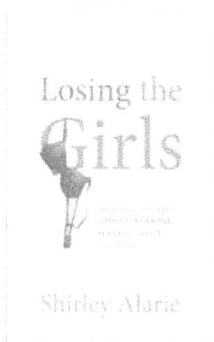

Losing the
Girls

Shirley Alarie

Installment 2

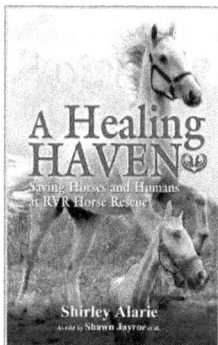

A Healing
HAVEN
Saving Horses and Humans
at RVR Horse Rescue

Shirley Alarie
as told by Shawn Jayroe et al.

True-life inspiration
From Rescue to Adoption

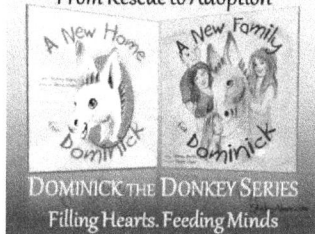

A New Home
Dominick

A New Family
Dominick

DOMINICK the DONKEY SERIES
Filling Hearts. Feeding Minds